WING SHOTS

Two black ducks

WING SHOTS

*A Series of Camera Studies of American
Game Birds and other Birds of Field
and Stream on the Wing*

by

ALBERT DIXON SIMMONS

Lyon, Mississippi
THE DERRYDALE PRESS

FOREWORD

Stalking the wary black duck at its home in the savannahs of Nova Scotia and patiently waiting for those whistling wings to come within camera range, carries with it all the thrill of the hunt—thus a study of a black duck in flight is bagged. Here too, that feathered summation of erratic speed in the air, the jacksnipe or Wilson's snipe, springs from under foot with a harsh "scaipe" and is away; a difficult target for camera or gun.

A great blue heron is "shot" on its way to a favorite fishing spot with neck tucked in, toes together in the rear and a pair of eyes that can spot a miniature camera in its case.

Tramping through woods of spruce and maple a sharp-shinned hawk announces that it has a nest near by starting a series of power dives on the intruder. It misses my hat but the fast lens records just how it uses its flight feathers.

A small island in the middle of a lake has its rookery of great black backed gulls. This looks like easy work but these are wary fellows even at nesting time. As the canoe draws near the old birds spiral and become just specks of white against a clear blue sky. From these gliding specks come the repeated message of "ha—ha—ha." Wise birds! and why not when they take four years to mature and live to be one hundred?

Along the sea shore—thanks to timely conservation laws—that once great game bird, the willet, nests again by the hundreds and becomes easy camera prey. A flock of sanderling swings over the waves and a greater yellow legs is whistled in to alight close enough to catch those graceful wings in action.

The greatest thrill of the hunt comes on Lake Erie—the migration of whistling swan. "Like huge arrows shot through heaven passed the swan." Then comes the fall migration of ducks gathering their numbers along their routes to the east and west of Hudson's Bay converging funnel like, at the western end of Lake Erie. Bluebill, mallard, pintail, teal, black duck, coot, spoonbill, whistler, bufflehead, speeding through the air, circling high in the clouds or with wings set, dropping into the feeding ground; all are sights that etch memory pictures for those whose province is the out-doors. This nucleus of our game bird population must be conserved, else our children or perhaps we ourselves will be heard to say: "Too bad that so many of our game birds have made their last flight to join the passenger pigeon."

It is hoped that the "wing shots" on the following pages will give the reader some of the many thrills that were the good fortune of the man behind the candid camera.

A.D.S.

May, 1936

LIST OF ILLUSTRATIONS

1 BLACK DUCKS (*frontispiece*)
In the early morning sun the white under parts of their wings flicker like a heliograph.

2 STUDY OF A BLACK DUCK

3 BLACK DUCK
Throttle wide open leaving me behind.

4 JACKSNIPE—WILSON'S SNIPE
Springs from under foot with a harsh "scaipe."

5 JACKSNIPE
A phantom like target for camera or gun.

6 GREAT BLUE HERON
With neck tucked in and toes together in the rear.

7 GREAT BLUE HERON
Getting away to a slow start with a wing spread of six feet.

8 GREAT BLUE HERON

9 SHARP SHINNED HAWK
I thought the power dive would end in the camera.

10 YOUNG SHARP SHINNED HAWKS
A nest full of bird eaters.

11 PORTRAIT OF A YOUNG BLACK BACKED GULL
They take four years to mature and live to be one hundred.

12 WILLET
Its flight reveals wing markings of rare beauty.

13 WILLET
"Pill—will—willet."

14 WILLET
Timely conservation laws are restoring this species once almost extinct.

15 SANDERLING
Apparently without leadership they dash and swirl over waves and rocks in close flying bunches.

16 GREATER YELLOW LEGS
Whistled in to alight almost at my feet.

17 KINGFISHER
He missed the minnow.

18 WHISTLING SWAN
"Like huge arrows shot through heaven,
Passed the swan."

19 WHISTLING SWAN
Scaling down with wings set and necks flexed.

20 WHISTLING SWAN FEEDING
They hold their necks erect.

21 MORNING FLIGHT

22 DUCKS OVER THE MARSHES
A mixed flock over the cat-tails and against the clouds, brought me a rare opportunity.

23 DUCKS AGAINST THE SKY

24 DUCKS IN DROPPING FLIGHT
Against a stiff wind they were side slipping to lose altitude.

25 DRIFTING DOWN

26 GREEN HERON
Its outline reminds me of some Japanese paintings.

27 HIGH FLYERS

28 BLUEBILLS—GREATER SCAUP
Unorganized flight.

29 LONE BLUEBILL

30 BLUEBILLS
They like the open water.

31 MALLARD
The ancestor of many kinds of domestic ducks.

32 MALLARD

33 MALLARD

34 MALLARD

35 MALLARD

36 MALLARD

37 PAIR OF MALLARDS

38 DRAKE MALLARD

39 AMERICAN BITTERN
   1 *On the limb*
   2 *Get set*
   3 *Go.*
     Just four seconds for three "shots."

40 PINTAIL

  Landing technique has its variations.

41 PINTAIL

  Using its wings, tail and feet to regain equilibrium when thrown off balance landing against a very heavy wind.

42 CLOSE FLYING PINTAIL

  All wings set for landing.

43 STUDY OF A PINTAIL

44 SANDUSKY MARSHES

45 TEAL

  Over the rushes at sixty miles per hour.

46 TEAL

  A few seconds later I heard the "swish" of landing.

47 BLUE WINGED TEAL

  Springs into the air with amazing speed.

48 BLUE WINGED TEAL

  The fastest flyers of the duck family.

49 GREEN WINGED TEAL

  Through the rushes—the bantams of the duck family.

50 GREEN WINGED TEAL

51 COOT

  "Skittering" to the take off.

52 COOT TAKING OFF

53 SPOONBILL

  His bill gives him away.

54 SHOVELLER

55 WHISTLER

  I heard the whistle of its wings before I saw it.

56 BUFFLEHEAD

  Fast wingers—their passion for wooden decoys has been their downfall.

57 MERGANSERS

  Their cylindrical bills give them an elongated appearance in flight.

58 MERGANSER

59 A MIXED FLOCK

  Blue and green winged teal, black duck, and pintail together during the fall migration.

60 BLACK TERN

  The "slough swallow" of the northwest.

61 BLACK TERN

62 EVENING FLIGHT
   I got away from sky lines of squares and rectangles.
63 CANADA GOOSE
   A wing spread of over six feet.
64 CANADA GEESE
65 CANADA GEESE
66 CANADA GEESE
67 CANADA GEESE
68 CANADA GEESE
   Pioneers of formation flying.
69 CANADA GEESE
70 CANADA GEESE
   Lucky number.
71 CANADA GEESE
   In straight line formation—one goose has lost a few flight feathers to the gunners but is holding its position in the line.
72 CANADA GEESE
73 HERRING GULL
   The graceful curvature of its wings in rising flight is most striking at this angle.
74 GREAT BLACK BACKED GULL
75 BONAPARTE'S GULL
   One of the smallest of the gull family.
76 BONAPARTE'S GULLS
77 BONAPARTE'S GULL
78 BONAPARTE'S GULL
79 MOURNING DOVE
   Jumped from a favorite roosting place in a pine tree.
80 PHEASANT
81 TREE SWALLOW
   A hollow metal fence post furnished a safe nesting place in the marshes.
82 CHIMNEY SWIFT
   This little fellow is streamlined for speed and can easily outdistance the fastest express train.
83 FINIS

WING SHOTS

Study of a black duck

©Albert J. Swanson

Frightened black duck

Jacqueline   Albert P. Simons

Jacksnipe – Wilson's snipe

Great blue heron #3

Great blue heron rising

Great blue heron

© Albert D. Cousins

Power dive - sharp shinned hawk

© Robert D Summers

Young sharp shinned hawks

Young black backed gull

Willet

"Pill – will – willet"

Willet   Albert D Sumin

Wing study of sanderling   ©Albert D. Summer

© Albert J. Simmons

Greater yellowlegs alighting

Kingfisher after dive

Whistling swan

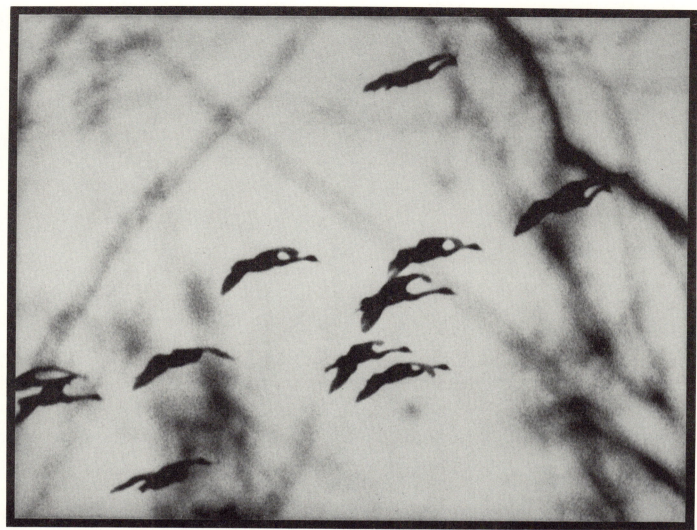

Swan scaling down

Wild swan feeding

Morning flight.

© Albert D. Summers

A mixed flock

Ducks against the sky

Pintail-chopping flight

©Robert P. Simmons

Drifting down

Green Heron

High flyers   Albert D. Summers

Flight of bluebells #2

© Albret D Sumn

Lone bluebill   ©Herbert D. Simon

Flight of bluebills #1

©Albert D. Sioux

Mallard

Study of a mallard

© Albert J. Sommer

Mallard alighting

Single mallard landing

©Hilbert D. Sumner

Mallard alighting

Albert D Lewis

Mallard alighting

Albert D Lumn

Pair of mallards

Albert D Lummin

Drake mallard - finis

On the limb -

Get set —

Go!

Pintail dropping in

Drake pintail in wind

Chinese flying pintail

Study of a pintail

©Robert H. Sounds

Sandusky marshes

Fast flying teal

Lone teal

Blue winged teal springing

Albert D. Summit

Blue winged teal

Green winged teal thru bushes

Green winged teal

Coot skittering

Coot taking off.

Shoveller

Shoveller

Whistler

Flight of Buffleheads

Albert F. Sonnen

Pair of mergansers

Merganser   Albert J. Swann

Wings against the wind

Black tern

Black tern

Evening flight

Robert D. Summers

Flight study of Canada goose.

Canada geese #1

© Albert T. Simon

Canada geese #2

Canada geese #3   Albert J. Simmons

Canada geese #4

Canada geese #5   ©Gilbert T. Simmons

Canada geese #6   Albert P. Simian

Lucky number (Canada geese)

Canada Geese #7   ©Albert P. Simmons

Canada geese #8   © Albert R. Germain

Herring gull

Great black backed gull. by Herbert T. [signature]

Bonaparte gull   Albert P. Simmins

Bonaparte gulls

Bonaparte gull

Bonaparte gull

Mourning dove

Albert D. Simms

Pheasant

Tree swallow

Chimney swift

Top speed 200 M.P.H. !

Finis   Ansel Adams

LIFTED UP

LIFTED UP

CRUCIFIXION, RESURRECTION
AND COMMUNITY IN JOHN

Thomas H. Olbricht

Cover art by Mandie Tepe

www.covenantpublishing.com

P.O. Box 390 Webb City, Missouri 64870
Call toll free at 877.673.1015

Library of Congress Cataloging-in-Publication Data
Olbricht, Thomas H.
Lifted up: crucifixion, resurrection, and community in John / Thomas Olbricht.
    p. cm.
Includes bibliographical references.
ISBN 1-892435-49-7 (pbk.)
1. Bible. N.T. John. XVIII-XX—Commentaries. Title.
BS2615.53.043 2005
226.5'07—dc22
                    2005007711

This book is dedicated to
Jerry Rushford, former student, colleague and friend.
Jerry is the consummate lectureship director.
His dedicated and meticulous care for this lectureship
has lifted it up so as to position it as
indispensable in the kingdom's work.

TABLE OF CONTENTS

INTRODUCTION   PAGE 9

CHAPTER 1   PAGE 11
John, A Unique Gospel

CHAPTER 2   PAGE 19
"Lifted Up"—The Thematic Seam in John's Gospel

CHAPTER 3   PAGE 35
Glorification Anticipated and the Disciples Charged
(John 11-17)

CHAPTER 4   PAGE 43
The Arrest and Jewish Trial of Jesus
(John 18:1-27)

CHAPTER 5   PAGE 55
The Trial Before Pilate
(John 18:28–19:16a)

CHAPTER 6   PAGE 69
The Lifting Up and Taking down to Be Lifted Up Again
(John 19:16b-42)

CHAPTER 7   PAGE 79
Lifted from the Tomb
(John 20:1-31)

CHAPTER 8   PAGE 95
Concluding Matters: The Appearance in Galilee
(John 21)

CHAPTER 9   PAGE 107
Why Ponder over the Gospel of John?

BIBLIOGRAPHY ON
THE GOSPEL OF JOHN   PAGE 117

ABOUT THE AUTHOR   PAGE 127

*God has a sustained relationship
with the universe he has made
and has revealed himself to humankind
through his Son, Jesus Christ.*

Introduction

Faith in these times, as in all times, must be sustained by the good news of what God has done in Christ. That news must constantly be recounted and embraced. That is why John wrote his Gospel. "Blessed are those who have not seen and yet have come to believe" (John 20:29).

The Christian explanation as to why there is something rather than nothing is that God exists and is the creator of all that is. Furthermore God has a sustained relationship with the universe he has made and has revealed himself to humankind through his Son, Jesus Christ. "No one has ever seen God. It is God the only Son, who is close to the Father's heart, who has made him known" (John 1:18). Not only is Jesus the revealer of God, he is God's means of salvation for all of humankind whenever they come to believe that Jesus is the Christ the Son of God. The affirmation that he is savior is especially disclosed in his being lifted upon the cross. "For God so loved the world that he gave his only Son, so that everyone who believes in him may not perish but may have eternal life" (John 3:16). **"And I, when I am lifted up from the earth, will draw all people to myself"** (John 12:32).

By taking seriously the message
of this great Gospel we enter
"abundant life in his name"

John,
A Unique Gospel

It is a great privilege to reflect upon the Gospel of John, especially in regard to the narratives on the death, resurrection, and appearances of the risen Lord. My own coming to an awareness of the significance of the Gospel of John may be of help as the reader takes up this book. This Gospel, by intention, buoys up the reader on the journey of faith. "But these are written so that you may come to believe that Jesus is the Messiah, the Son of God, and that through believing you may have life in his name" (John 20:31).

I was a college junior at what is now Northern Illinois University and preaching for the recently founded Church of Christ in DeKalb when I first started reading the Gospel of John seriously. I didn't grow up as a Bible reader though I read periodically and listened to my mother's frequent reading aloud from the Bible storybooks. We went to church whenever it assembled so I heard many sermons and the Bible as it was taught in adult classes. I don't recall, however, sitting in on a class in which a Gospel was studied. I recall studies on Acts, Ephesians, 1 and 2 Timothy, 1 Corinthians, Genesis and Exodus, but no study of the Gospels.

I heard Matthew quoted often by the preachers and teachers, sometimes from the Sermon on the Mount but especially from sections in which Jesus' condemned the Pharisees and others for failure to keep his word. Two frequently heard quotes were:

> "Not everyone who says to me, 'Lord, Lord,' will enter the kingdom of heaven, but only the one who does the will of my Father in heaven. On that day many will say to me, 'Lord, Lord, did we not prophesy in your name, and cast out demons in your name, and do many deeds of power in your name?' Then I will declare to them, 'I never knew you; go away from me, you evildoers'" (Matt. 7:21-23).

11

"But woe to you, scribes and Pharisees, hypocrites! For you lock people out of the kingdom of heaven. For you do not go in yourselves, and when others are going in, you stop them. Woe to you, scribes and Pharisees, hypocrites! For you cross sea and land to make a single convert, and you make the new convert twice as much a child of hell as yourselves" (Matt. 23:13-15).

I did not hear John cited much. Occasionally I heard John 3:16, "For God so loved the world that he gave his only Son, so that everyone who believes in him may not perish but may have eternal life." Our preachers much preferred to quote Acts 2:38. "Peter said to them, 'Repent, and be baptized every one of you in the name of Jesus Christ so that your sins may be forgiven; and you will receive the gift of the Holy Spirit.'" I heard sermons on Nicodemus and the statement of Jesus to him, "Verily, verily, I say unto thee, Except a man be born of water and of the Spirit, he cannot enter into the kingdom of God" (John 3:5 KJV). I heard comparisons of the church and Christians to the vine and branches in John 15, and I occasionally listened to a sermon on John 17 that emphasized Jesus' prayer that his disciples be one. But I had never studied John with any intensity. I took a course on the Gospels from Andy T. Ritchie Jr. at Harding College (now University), but I don't recall much time spent with the Gospel of John. I mostly recall an in-depth study of the Sermon on the Mount.

I first gave more attention to John in 1950, since this Gospel was a central focus of Scripture study on WMBI, Chicago, the radio station of the Moody Bible Institute, and of the evangelicals on the campus of Northern, especially the InterVarsity Christian Fellowship. In 1949 I transferred from Harding to Northern Illinois in DeKalb, Illinois, so as to preach for a congregation I helped start in the summer of 1948. People who participated in InterVarsity Christian with some frequency distributed on campus individual copies of the Gospel of John. They considered John the primary document in the Bible for opening the door so as to encourage the unconverted to receive the Christian faith. As evidence of its value for reaching unbelievers they cited, John 20:30-31, "Now Jesus did many other signs in the presence of his disciples, which are not written in this book. But these are written so that you may come to believe that Jesus is the Messiah, the Son of God, and that through believing you may have life in his name."

I hoped to share their excitement over this Gospel to bring about conversions, but I had difficulty. I perceived Acts to be a much better introduction to conversion from a New Testament perspective. If a Gospel were to be read I thought that Matthew and Luke were much more direct and likely more suitable for securing interest and comprehension. During that time I learned that scholars noted the differences in John when compared with Matthew, Mark and Luke. The latter three were designed the Synoptics (from the Greek, that may be translated, "look a likes") because they are much more similar to each other than to John.

In my view, though Matthew and Luke seemed much like the other prose I read in and out of the classroom, John was different. I didn't fully know what to make of it. I was somewhat put off with the style of John which in the King James seemed abstract and sometimes abrupt, if not archaic. John frequently referred to the Word, life, eternal life, light, darkness, the world, flesh, glory, grace, testimony, the lamb of God, time, hour, sign, born from above, from below, purification, living water, works, judgment, bread, sheepfold, gate, other sheep, the Comforter or Advocate, the vine and branches, and various other words and conceptions. These seemed to have some special meaning of which I was in some cases not altogether clear.

I missed the narrative features of Matthew and Luke in which Jesus went from one place to another with some description of settings as he traveled. I missed the pithy sayings of the Sermon on the Mount. But perhaps most of all I missed the parables which if not enlightening were the bases for trying to settle certain kinds of anomalies in Jesus' teaching. One finds the parables of the good Samaritan (10:29-37), the prodigal son (15:11-32), and the rich man and Lazarus (16:19-31) only in Luke. In John may be discovered many more discourses and lengthy exhortations introducing arguments that are sometimes difficult to follow.

I was perplexed by numerous statements in the Gospel of John not found in the Synoptics. Why was the water changed to wine in John 2:6, water the Jews used for purification? What did Jesus mean by being born again, or born from above 3:3? Did Jesus mean that believers must literally eat his flesh and drink his blood 6:54? Who are the sheep not of this fold 10:16? Why was it "time" for Jesus to be glorified when some Greeks expressed to the disciples their wish to see Jesus 12:20-23? How was it possible that the disciples would do greater works than did Jesus 14:12? Who was the disciple Jesus loved 13:23?

It took me some time to learn to appreciate John. Some from early Christian times suggested that John was a spiritual and theological presentation of the story of Jesus. Matthew, Mark and Luke in contrast were more focused upon historical narrative. I knew John was different but I didn't find this distinction particularly helpful. It seemed to me that all the Gospels were focused upon God and his Son, Jesus Christ. In that sense, they were all theological. But John contained theology expressed differently. It was not until I started teaching John in New Testament Theology at Abilene Christian in 1969 that I began to appreciate the Gospel. After reading in it seriously and examining various commentaries, especially the work of Raymond Brown, it dawned on me that John more than any of the other Gospels contained trajectories of vocabulary and thought that were different from the Synoptics but consistent throughout the Gospel. These perspectives invited the reader to struggle with "hidden" and double meanings. John through these insights became a delight and a challenge.

Now I find the Gospel of John a witness to the risen and ascended Jesus in its own right. More than in the other Gospels one is invited by the author to trace trajectories throughout the Gospel, such as the significance in Jesus as the one from above who leads readers to a birth from above (John 3:3). Another trajectory is Jesus' hour, that is, when in the course of his ministry his time arrives (John 2:4; 12:23). One is also invited to look behind obvious events for hidden meanings, for example, Nathanael seeing the "heaven opened and the angels of God ascending and descending upon the Son of Man" (John 1:51). And Jesus saying to his mother regarding the disciple he loved, "Woman, here is your son" (John 19:26) and to the disciple regarding his mother, "Here is your mother" (John 19:27). To take up the reading of John and to contemplate the depths of its meaning are both instructive and faith building. By taking seriously the message of this great Gospel we enter "abundant life in his name" (John 10:10; 20:31).

THE SIGNIFICANCE OF JOHN 18–20

What is there about Jesus of Nazareth that makes him different from every other person? The answer of his early followers was that he was the Son of God, and that he died, arose again, and ascended into heaven to be with God. It was not until all of these actions occurred that the disciples commenced writing down their convictions about him. It may seem unusual to write a book about the last part of the Gospel of John that focuses upon the crucifixion, resurrection of Jesus and his contacts with the disciples following his resurrection. But it was these events that finally convinced the disciples of his significance and his claim to be the only begotten of God. It was a description of these events that were first recorded by the disciples. The words and works apparently were added at a later time. These events reach into the heart of Jesus' ministry. For this reason a focus on the last four chapters of the Gospel of John cuts to the heart of the good news regarding Jesus of Nazareth.

The part of the Gospels having to do with the crucifixion is designated the passion narrative by scholars. The word Greek word pascho from which we obtain "passion" in English is normally translated suffering, and therefore the reason for this labeling. The passion narrative in the Gospel of John is located in 18–19, chapter 20 concerns the resurrection while chapter 21 is often considered an appendix or added discourse. Regardless, the material in chapter 21 picks up on several trajectories in the rest of the Gospel.

Regarding the passion narrative, Raymond Brown, who published a major two-volume work on these narratives in all the four Gospels, wrote,

> The Passion Narrative, as it proceeds from arrest through trial to condemnation, execution, and burial (thus from Gethsemane to the grave), constitutes in each Gospel the longest consecutive action recounted of Jesus. Aesthetically, more than any other section of the Gospels, indeed even more than the infancy narrative, it has cap-

tured the attention and imagination of dramatists (passion plays), artists, and musicians. Literally, passion vignettes have left their mark on language and imagery: thirty pieces of silver, Judas kiss, cockcrow, washing one's hands of blood. Historically, Jesus' death was the most public moment of his life as figures known from Jewish or secular history (Caiaphas, Annas, Pilate) crossed his path. Indeed, alongside "born of the virgin Mary," the other phrase that made its way into the creed, "suffered under Pontius Pilate," has become a marker anchoring Christian belief about the Son of God to a Jesus who was a human figure of actual history.[1]

The events leading to the death of Christ have once again come to the forefront through Mel Gibson's, attendance-breaking cinema, *The Passion of the Christ*. Gibson contends that he mainly drew upon the Gospels of the New Testament for the details of this movie, and so he has in many features. The Gospel writers, however, did not see the need to offer such a vivid description of the scourging, the nailing, the violence, the physical pain and the emaciation of these climatic days. Gibson and his supporting crew added specific details not found in the Gospels and drew upon medieval traditions that exerted concentrated effort to dramatize the details. Gibson admitted to drawing specifically upon the visions of Austrian Anne Catherine Emmerich (1774–1824) as recorded by Clemens Bretano.[2]

Various authors in medieval times through prayer and meditation manuals sought to bring devotees to a deeper commitment to Christ through an imaginative presentation of his incredible suffering and hideous death. It was argued that these embellished depictions were highly desirable even if not contained in the early accounts. Those who entered emotionally into these details

[1] Brown, Raymond, *The Death of the Messiah: From Gethsemane to the Grave: A Commentary on the Passion Narratives in the Four Gospels.* (Garden City, NY: Doubleday, 1994) 1:vii.

[2] Emmerich, Anna Katharina, *The life of Our Lord and Saviour Jesus Christ : combined with The bitter passion, and The life of Mary / From the revelations of Anna Catharina Emmerick as recorded in the journals of Clemens Brentano*, arranged and edited by Carl E. Schmöger, 4 vols. (Fresno: Academy Library Guild, 1954).

16

became convinced of their own role in Christ's death, developed a strong sense of their sinfulness and a sorrow for it, and were overwhelmed by Christ's redemptive activity. These medieval manuals held that any additional depictions not found in the Gospels that resulted in a love for God, Christ and fellow humans were warranted. These authors had a deep commitment to the view that the salvation of the believer depended upon empathetic meditation.[3]

John in his presentation of the passion narrative gives fewer insights into Christ's suffering as he met his death than the other Gospels, and even in these Gospels the depictions were far less vivid than in Gibson's movie. Surely someone who viewed these gruesome details first hand as did John could have accurately dramatized the horror if he had conceived these of benefit. He was not concerned, however, to weigh his readers down with heavy guilt and gore. He was eager to take up the story of the resurrection and the new life and hope that it made possible. He was not interested in a burden of guilt, and suffering. For him Jesus came to bring life and that more abundantly.

However one may react to *The Passion of the Christ*, it calls to our attention once again the significance of these last days of Jesus in contemplating the Christ story. In them the true meaning of Jesus' ministry is disclosed. That humans reacted so bloodily and violently to Jesus' words and works is a vital part of the story. Gibson, at minimum, has appropriately honed in upon these consequential days and hours.

---

[3] Amy Hollywood, "Kill Jesus" Harvard Divinity School Bulletin 53 (2004) 3:32-34.

The imagery of Jesus being lifted up
is a developed story line in John
long before we come to chapters 18-21.

"Lifted Up"
The Thematic Seam
in John's Gospel

2

It is important before we take up the chapters 18–20 of the Gospel that we understand the thematic threads of John's Gospel. The imagery of Jesus being lifted up is a developed story line in John long before we come to chapters 18–21. In the first instance we read, "And just as Moses lifted up the serpent in the wilderness, so must the Son of Man be lifted up, that whoever believes in him may have eternal life. 'For God so loved the world that he gave his only Son, so that everyone who believes in him may not perish but may have eternal life'" (John 3:14-16). Often the main occurrence that comes to mind when we think of Jesus being lifted up is, "'And I, when I am lifted up from the earth, will draw all people to myself.' He said this to indicate the kind of death he was to die. The crowd answered him, 'We have heard from the law that the Messiah remains forever. How can you say that the Son of Man must be lifted up? Who is this Son of Man?'" (John 12:32-34).

Running throughout the Gospel of John is the declaration that in Jesus' glorification his divine powers became transparent. The glorification of Jesus was in his being lifted up. The first disciples saw that glory (1:14) in his death (3:14-16; 8:27-29; 12:32-33), in his resurrection from the grave (11:25; 20:6-8), in his return to the Father (14:3; 20:17), and in the birth from above of those who believed (3:3; 17:20-23).

ON LOCATING THE THREADS
IN JOHN'S GOSPEL

How should we go about exploring the major trajectories in John? Should we first set out a scholarly introduction of the sort that is famous in modern commentaries? While this may be of help, I am going to proceed in a more direct manner. John wrote his Gospel to be read aloud, most likely to those who had already come to believe that Jesus is the Christ, the Son of God (John 20:31) as opposed to those who are hearing about Jesus for the first time. We will best understand the Gospel, in my view, therefore, not by proceeding according to a standard scholarly introduction, but by picking up the narrative as John sets it out.

John's Gospel, more than the Synoptics, introduces statements and incidents throughout that anticipate the work and word of Jesus from start to finish. It is for this reason that it is important for us to plunge right into the Gospel and into the tracking of these seams so that when we come to the passion narrative and ending (18–21) we will have some sense of what to anticipate in Jesus' final days. We will also have a more in-depth perspective and foundation for explicating these closing chapters.

JOHN, CHAPTER 1, PROLOGUE: THE SUBJECT OF JOHN'S "BIOGRAPHY"

John does not dilly dally as to the subject of his "biography." The significant person about whom he is writing is the Word who was at the beginning; The Word was with God; He is God (1:1). Now lest anyone has doubts as to the person under discussion, John declares, "The Word became flesh and lived among us" (1:14). The Word who came into the world with a God given assignment is Jesus, "the Lamb of God who takes away the sin of the world! (1:29). He created all being and beings. He authored everything that humans know about and experience, "Without him not one thing came into being" (1:3).

Jesus received a commission from God on behalf of the world he created. He came to reveal the divine life that is the light of all people (1:4). John tells his auditors later that Jesus, the Word, was sent by God. "He whom God has sent speaks the words of God" (John 3:34). But not only was he sent by God, he will return to God. "Jesus, knowing that the Father had given all things into his hands, and that he had come from God and was going to God, got up from the table" (13:3-4). Jesus had a God-given mission. He will return to God when his mission is complete. The final phase will be his glorification: his lifting up on the cross, from the tomb and in his ascension to the Father. His early followers beheld his glory "as of a father's only son, full of grace and truth" (1:14).

The God-decreed mission of Jesus almost immediately met with opposition and indifference. Jesus did not arrive incognito or unheralded! John, a man sent from God, announced his arrival. John declared that he was "not worthy to untie the thong of the sandal" (1:27) of Jesus, whom he was sent to announce. Jesus was in the world, but the world, even though he created it, did not recognize him for who he was (1:10). His own people did not accept him. His mission was fulfilled in those who were open. He gave them the power to "become children of God . . . because they were born of God" (1:12-13). Those who believed saw his glory, which glory was later declared to be his being lifted up. From Jesus, who was sent, believers received grace upon grace, that is, abundant and continuing grace. He was close to the heart of the Father and he made God known through his word and work (1:18).

The mission of Jesus was to make it possible for humans to be born from above and to receive forgiveness of sins in this world (1:4, 13, 29). The Spirit descended upon Jesus like a dove, and he in turn baptized believers with the Holy Spirit, and thus bestowed on them the life that comes from above (3:5). When Andrew followed Jesus home he was so impressed that he announced to his brother, Simon Peter, "We have found the Messiah" (1:41). The next day Jesus came upon Philip, and requested that he follow him. Philip was similarly impressed. He hurried to Nathanael and excitedly declared, "We have found him about whom Moses in the Law and also the prophets wrote" (1:46).

How was anyone to know he was the one from God? John announced who Jesus was. In addition, what he did and said pointed to God-given powers unavailable to mere humans. These "signs" pointed heavenward—the source of his abilities. The signs began with what Jesus said to Nathanael, "I saw you under the fig tree" (1:50). The two numbered signs are only in respect to signs in Cana. The first sign in Cana was at the wedding (2:11). The second sign in Cana was the healing of the son of a royal official (4:46, 54).[4] Incidentally, Nathanael was from Cana of Galilee (21:2). Jesus did many signs (2:23; 20:30) the greatest of all being his resurrection

---

[4] See my essay on the signs in the Gospel of John, "The Theology of the Signs in the Gospel of John," *Johannine Studies*, ed. James E. Priest (Malibu, CA: Pepperdine University Press, 1989).

from the dead "because I lay down my life in order to take it up again" (10:17). More than all else his resurrection was the sign that in him was life (1:4).

The sign is not the thing. Jesus' announcement to Nathanael that he saw him in advance was not God's Messiah. But that declaration pointed to the conclusion that the one uttering it was. As one drives west on Interstate 90 past the famous Wall Drug Store and approaches Rapid City, South Dakota, one sees a large sign on the right "Mt. Rushmore National Monument, next exit." But the sign is not the monument. The monument is the faces of George Washington, Thomas Jefferson, Abraham Lincoln and Theodore Roosevelt carved on Mt. Rushmore some twenty miles to the southwest. The sign is not the monument, but it points one in the right direction. The signs in John are not the Messiah, the Son of God. They, however, declare that what Jesus says and does is so unlike the words and deeds of mere humans that they come about, because in him—indeed a man—is God!

The signs that Jesus was from God can be seen in Jesus' words as well as in his deeds. Nathanael believed that Jesus was from God because Jesus said to him, "I saw you under the fig tree before Philip called you" (1:48-50). The woman at the well in Samaria declared that Jesus was the Messiah because he "told me everything I have ever done! He cannot be the Messiah, can he?" (4:29). The remark to Nathanael, however, pales in comparison to the greatest sign. "You will see heaven opened and the angels descending upon the Son of Man" (1:51).

Chapter 1 of John lays many foundations for what is to come. Jesus is God, and the only Son of God, but he became flesh and made God known. Through him all things were created. Jesus was announced by John the Baptist (who pointed his disciples to him) but rejected by most of his own people. To those who received him he gave the power to be born of God, to receive continuous grace and be baptized by the Holy Spirit. The death of Jesus for the sins of the world was also announced. Prospective disciples heralded Jesus as the Messiah, the prophet and the king of Israel.

JOHN, CHAPTERS 2–9, SIGNS, ENCOUNTERS AND CONFRONTATIONS WITH THE JEWS

It has become conventional among scholars to identify Chapters 2–12 in John's Gospel as the signs section iterating the signs pointing to Jesus as the Son of God and Messiah. These signs highlighted certain extraordinary feats of Jesus, constantly raising the question as to whether he was sent from God. They provided the initial evidences necessary for a developing faith. John declared that he depicted the signs Jesus did in writing so that "you may come to believe that Jesus is the Messiah, the Son of God, and that through believing you might have life through his name" (20:31). While the signs are exceedingly important, I think it is more insightful to divide John 2–17 into (1) Jesus' confrontations with the Jews—John 2–9, and (2) his teaching of the disciples—John 10–17. John 2–9 described Jesus' encounters with those who came to faith, but even more his confrontation by and with the Jewish leaders. In John 10–17 Jesus prepared his disciples for the continuation of his earthly mission.

Another major trajectory that runs through Chapters 2–9 sets forth the mission of Jesus. The signs gave credence to Jesus' mission. The mission of Jesus was to be glorified by being lifted up so that "everyone who believes in him may not perish but may have eternal life" (John 3:16). Jesus interacted with his disciples and his critics in Galilee and Jerusalem in preparation for his lifted-up glory (2–12). Jesus was not an accidental tourist. His mission was according to a timetable. He declared to his mother, who pointed out to him the insufficient wine supply, "My hour has not yet come" (2:4). When was Jesus' mission accomplished? It was accomplished when his hour to be glorified arrived. "The hour has come for the Son of Man to be glorified" (12:23). Jesus was glorified when he was lifted up. "And I, when I am lifted up from the earth, will draw all people to myself. He said this to indicate the kind of death he was to die" (12:32-33).

SIGNS AND FAITH

How is it that a sign brings about faith? The sign at the wedding in Cana is paradigmatic for comprehending the signs in John. The sign begins in an empirical word or action. It often commences from something on and of the earth. But it points beyond its earthly origins to those from above. The sign at the wedding centered upon the depleted and replenished wine. Before the replenishment, however, the declaration of a true believer—in this case Mary—provided a catalyst. "Do whatever he tells you" (2:5). In the second stage the water was changed to unbelievably good tasting wine. The water wasn't just any water. It was six large containers of water employed in Jewish rites in which the water is sprinkled on the one who seeks purification. That Jesus changed this ritual water to wine anticipates the purification that is soon to replace Jewish sprinkling. It is a new purification that results from the baptism of the water and the Spirit (3:5) based upon belief that Jesus is the Messiah (3:16) and through the drinking of the fruit of the vine—his blood (6:53). The third stage on the road to faith is the openness of the disciples to the prospect that Jesus can achieve the implausible. The disciples have been prepared for this openness by their rapprochement with Jesus and the confidence of Mary. Because of this revelation of Jesus' glory (2:11)—that he created the good wine by his Word—the disciples believed in him.

The coming to faith in which signs are involved continues according to these same four stages even into the present. Often a believing parent first points to Jesus. The child next hears of Jesus' uncommon feats. Third, openness on the part of the growing youth to the prospect that a divine source is the most likely explanation. Fourth, as the result, the young adult receives Jesus in faith.

In Chapter 2 we will pursue these signs and Jesus' confrontations with the Jews in John 2–9. In Chapter 3 we will scrutinize Jesus' discourses as he anticipates the final aspects of being lifted up. His anticipation gives special attention to the continuation and expansion of his mission in the circle of his disciples.

JESUS AND THE RELIGIOUS LEADERS
(2:12–9:41)

Jesus came into discussion and often conflict with the esteemed religious leadership in Jerusalem, Samaria and Galilee. He initiated a series of conversations with the temple authorities at the Passover (2:12-25); with Nicodemus a Pharisee (3:1-21); the woman at the well in Samaria (4:1-45); Jewish leadership at the unknown festival (5:1-47); Jews in Galilee (6:1-71); at the Feast of Booths in Jerusalem

(7:1–8:59); and those critical of his healing the blind man (9:1-41).

JESUS WITH TEMPLE AUTHORITIES AT THE PASSOVER
(2:12-25)

Jesus, through whom everything that was made was made, clearly produced the materials from which the temple was built. He gave life to the religious functionaries who operated and protected the temple, but they did not know him. On his first visit to the temple in John, Jesus drove away the money-changers. He charged that they were making his Father's house a "marketplace" (2:16). Jesus got the attention of the temple officials. To put Jesus on the spot they challenged him to show a sign. Jesus declared, "Destroy this temple and in three days I will raise it up" (2:19). The sign was too cryptic for the officials to make sense of, and also even for the disciples. The disciples remembered the sign and believed in him even more after he was **lifted up!** (2:22). This sign, as the one to Nathanael and to the woman at the well in Samaria, was a word of Jesus not an action, nevertheless it came to fruition in the future death and resurrection of Jesus. That event was the major sign in John as to Jesus' identity and mission. The words of Jesus turned out to be signs because he "knew what was in everyone" (2:25) for he was the Word through whom all things were made. He anticipated the questions both of Nathanael and the Samaritan woman, with the result that his observations were prophetic.

NICODEMUS A PHARISEE
(3:1-21)

Nicodemus heard of the signs that Jesus did, and even declared that they must be from God, but still he did not believe that Jesus was God (3:1-2). He was not yet open to that prospect (3:9-10). Nicodemus did not comprehend being born from above. Jesus declared that the one born from above must be "born of water and the Spirit" (3:5). The one baptism (Eph. 4:5) has two aspects, the water and the Spirit (Rom. 6:3-4; 1 Cor. 12:13). The Greek word translated in the NRSV "above" can also be translated "again," but the best translation in this case is "above" since it is a birth from the Spirit (see also John 1:33). The emphasis is on

God's act, not on the faith of the believer. Those who relish conversion as being born again sometimes stress the receptiveness of the believer rather than the work of the Spirit.

While some minimize the work of the Spirit, others downplay the importance of the water. It seems strange to deny baptism in water in John. John the Baptist, who paved the way for Jesus, baptized with water (John 1:26), and he preferred Aenon near Salim because there was much water there (John 3:23). Jesus and his disciples' baptized with water (John 3:26) in the same manner as John. Whether Jesus himself baptized is another matter (John 4:2).

Jesus reiterated that he was on a mission from above—he has descended and will ascend (3:13). His mission will be accomplished when he is lifted up like the serpent in the wilderness (3:14). The only Son of God came into the world so that "whoever believes in him may have eternal life" (3:16). The "world" in John most often refers to those persons who reject the rule of God; they are alienated from him.[5] Yet in his great love God gave his only Son for those who stood over against him! The prospect for eternal life has one source—belief that God sent his lifted-up Son. At the same time destruction comes upon those who do not believe in the Son (3:17-21). In John it is either live or die. Believe and live—fail to believe and perish!

Beasley-Murray wrote:

> The concept of the "lifting up" of Christ occurs for the first time in our passage [John 3:14-17]. Exaltation and glorification are intertwined in this Gospel in a manner unique in the NT. Whereas other writers view the death of Jesus as deepest humiliation, reversed by the divine action in raising him on high (Philippians 2:6-11), the Evangelist sees the death on the cross as itself participation in the glorification of Jesus…It is the end result of the Evangelist's seeing the cross and resurrection of Jesus as *one redemptive event*.[6]

---

[5] See my essay, Thomas H. Olbricht, "Its Works are Evil (John 7:7)," *Restoration Quarterly*, 7:4 (1963), pp. 242-244.

[6] Beasley-Murray, George Raymond, 1916, *John*, 2nd edition (Nashville: Thomas Nelson Publishers, 1999), p. 54.

Toward the end of chapter 3 John fleshes out items he has introduced earlier. John the Baptist declared to the Pharisees who asked about his identity, that he was not worthy to untie the thong of the sandal of the one to follow. In a later utterance to his own disciples, John declared, when they reported that Jesus was baptizing more disciples, "He must increase, but I must decrease" (John 3:30).

THE WOMAN AT THE WELL IN SAMARIA AND THE RESIDENTS OF THE REGION (4:1-45)

The story of the woman at the well in Samaria is another case of Jesus amazing people with what he knows about them. His prescience becomes a sign pointing to a reality beyond the immediate concrete entity at hand. Jesus began his conversation with the woman by making a comment on the water in Jacob's well. Beginning with a physical entity Jesus often redirected those with whom he came in contact to an analogically, heavenly reality. He offered the woman living water that would gush up to eternal life (John 4:14). The woman was not clear as to what that was all about, but when Jesus brought up her many husbands she was convinced that he was no ordinary Jew. She asked herself, then reported to her own people that he might be the Messiah (John 4:25, 29). She served as a catalyst for their coming to faith (4:39).

As Jesus discoursed with the woman at the well, for the first time he identified himself as *egō eimi* (4:26; see the explanation of the translator in the footnotes of your Bible). By this language Jesus in the Gospel of John identified himself with the God who appeared to Abraham, Isaac and Jacob. When the Samaritan woman entertained the possibility that Jesus was the Messiah, and asked him point blank, he responded, "*egō eimi*" which literally translated simply states "I am." When Moses asked God for his name as he stood facing the burning bush, God answered, "I AM WHO I AM" (in the Septuagint translation, *egō eimi ho on*, Exod. 3:14). In effect then, Jesus identified himself as the I AM who appeared to Moses, that is, God himself.

Many people in Jesus' time would have made this connection because they heard Exodus read in the Greek Septuagint translation, even in Palestine. In an additional four incidents Jesus employed the same construction. In John 8:24 he told the Pharisees who criticized him, "you will die in your sins unless you believe that I am. . . ." In other words unless people believe that Jesus is identical with the one who appeared at the burning bush, they will die in their sins. In John 8:28 Jesus told the same group, "When you have lifted up the Son of Man, then you will realize that I am. . . ." The Jesus who died on the cross will rise to live again. In the Gospel of John, Jesus laid down his life in order that he himself could take it up. "I have power to lay it down, and I have power to take it up again" (John 10:18). Jesus attributed the very amazing powers of God to himself. In John 8:56 Jesus declared boldly to the Jews that Abraham rejoiced and was glad that he had seen his day. They chided him for implying that he had seen Abraham. Jesus then put it stronger, "Very truly, I tell you, before Abraham was, I am" (John 8:58). In this statement he declared his existence prior to Abraham, and his single identity with God. Finally, Jesus stated plainly that one of the twelve sitting at table with him was going to betray him. Jesus declared that he was telling the disciples in advance so they would apprehend his prior knowledge regarding events yet to transpire, that is, the powers of God himself. "I tell you this now, before it occurs, so that when it does occur, you may believe that I am. . . . " (John 13:19). John declared, "In the beginning was the Word, and the Word was with God, and the Word was God" (John 1:1). Jesus identified himself in the same manner as the God who appeared to Moses at the burning bush.

JEWISH LEADERSHIP AT THE UNKNOWN FESTIVAL
(5:1-47)

In several incidents in chapters 5 through 12 Jesus entered into discussion with Jewish officials in regard to his person and mission. John (chapter 5) reports a second journey of Jesus to Jerusalem, in this case, to an unknown festival. Jesus healed a paralytic who was unable to reach the pool at the Sheep Gate when it stirred. The paralytic did not know at first it was Jesus. When the Jews asked him who healed him, he responded that he did not know. But Jesus stayed around and the man found out who he was. He now reported to the Jews that it was Jesus. The Jews immediately turned upon

Jesus because he healed on the Sabbath (5:16). Jesus responded that his mission was to accomplish deeds identical to those of God. He added that the critics will be astounded by far greater works, because, "the Father raises the dead and gives them life, so also the Son gives life to whomever he wishes" (5:21).

Jesus now launched into a discourse in which he declared that his mission is to give life to all those who will listen to the voice of the Son of Man (5:28, 29). He came not to do his own will, "but the will of him who sent me" (5:30). He avowed that being sent was affirmed by testimony other than his own. The testimony came from (1) John the Baptist (5:33), (2) the works the Father gave him to do (5:36), (3) the Father (5:37), and (4) the Scriptures (5:39). The Jews held from ancient times that the chief purpose of the Scripture is that in them the way to eternal life may be discovered. Jesus contended that rather the Scriptures pointed to him who was the source of life. He accused the leaders of rejecting the available testimony because they did not have the love of the Father, nor did they believe Moses (5:42-47).

JEWS IN GALILEE
(6:1-71)

On his return to Galilee Jesus responded to the hunger of five thousand people. He gave thanks for five barley loaves and two fish, and from these the five thousand ate their fill. When they gathered up what remained it came to twelve baskets. Jesus demonstrated tangibly by his word of prayer that he had the capability of making everything that is made. The people concluded, as the result of Jesus' remarkable powers, that he was a prophet (6:14).

Jesus feared that the crowd would take him by force and make him king (6:14). But it was not his hour to be designated king at that time, so he withdrew to a mountain. Eventually Jesus was proclaimed king of the Jews by no less than Pilate even if in contempt. That was really who Jesus was. Nathanael anticipated his authentic, though hidden identity, at the start of the Gospel. "Nathanael replied, "Rabbi, you are the Son of God! You are the King of Israel!" (John 1:49). On the Sea of Galilee with the disciples, Jesus, in the midst of the storm reassured them, "I am (Gr. *egō eimi*); do not be afraid" proclaiming himself the exodus God (6:20). The creator of the storm is able to control the storm as well as protect those who are his in its midst.

Those who had eaten the loaves and fishes followed Jesus even though he took a boat to the other side of the lake. Jesus chided them by alleging that they sought him, not because they saw the signs but because they ate their fill of the loaves (6:26). It is clear from the Gospel of John that the signs only produce faith and the life that follows, when people are open to and accept the one to whom the signs point, that is, Jesus, the "I am." The mission of Jesus was not in order that people would stop and marvel at the signs he was able to do. Those who followed around the lake were not interested in the one to whom the sign pointed, but only the sign itself, that is, the bread. It were as if, upon seeing the sign "Mt. Rushmore National Monument," the passerby stopped and took a picture of the sign, and went on her way without standing before the mountain and viewing the replicas of the presidents carved there. In our time some are so excited about what they perceive to be charismatic gifts that they place faith in them, and not so much in the Son of God. John is clear that the signs are of consequence only to those who believe in the Word, that is Jesus. "This is the work of God that you believe in him whom he has sent" (6:29).

John announced in 1:4 that Jesus came to share the life that resided in him. Now Jesus proclaimed that the bread he provided "comes down from heaven and gives life to the world" (6:33). This bold declaration of Jesus created criticism among the Jews. They were by no means open to his heavenly connection. "Is this not Jesus, the son of Joseph?" (6:42). Jesus added to the consternation when he insisted that, "the bread that I will give for the life of the world is my flesh" (6:51). He compounded the puzzlement when he avowed, "unless you eat the flesh of the Son of Man and drink his blood, you have no life in you" (6:53). In these remarks the Lord's Supper is anticipated. The result was many of the disciples who regularly went about with Jesus turned back. Jesus charged that they would be even more offended when they saw him lifted up, in this case, ascending to where he was before (6:62). Then Jesus turned to the twelve and asked if they would also go away. Peter declared that Jesus only had the words to life because he was the "Holy One of God" (6:69).

30

JESUS AT THE FEAST OF
BOOTHS IN JERUSALEM
(7:1-8:59)

In the seventh chapter Jesus' brothers, who did not believe him to be from God, challenged him to go to Jerusalem for the feast of booths and demonstrate his powers. Jesus rejected their suggestion because his time had not yet arrived—that is, his being lifted up. Being lifted up (on the cross, from the grave, and to God) culminated his mission. Jesus, after rejecting his brothers' proposal, later went to Jerusalem in secret (7:10). In the middle of the festival he began teaching in the temple. The Jews demanded to know how he exhibited such learning when he had not been taught as they.

John often uses the designation "Jews" when the Synoptics refer to scribes and Pharisees, and sometimes teachers of the law. A widely accepted hypothesis now is that the Gospel of John was written at such a time as Christians were being forced out of synagogues so that the opponents of Jesus were simply identified as Jews.[7] The generic identification of the opponents as Jews is not an indication of racial prejudice, since Jesus, a Jew, frequented the temple during the feasts. Jesus responds to his Jewish questioners, "My teaching is not mine but his who sent me" (7:15). Jesus charged the Jews with threatening to kill him, and residents in Jerusalem suspected as much (7:25). Indeed the Jews attempted his arrest (7:30). Many, even in Jerusalem, were convinced that he was the Messiah because of the signs he did (7:31). But it was not yet time for Jesus to be lifted up (7:30). In this context Jesus mentioned for the first time the Holy Spirit he planned to bestow when he was lifted up, that is, glorified (7:39). It was only after Jesus was raised that he breathed the Holy Spirit upon the disciples (John 20:22).

In chapter 8 Jesus has a long discussion with the Jews over who he is, that is, the one sent from the Father (8:18). He charged "You know neither me nor my Father" (8:19). Though Jesus kept talking they still resisted belief. At that point Jesus highlighted an event that would later disclose his identity. "When you have lifted up the Son of Man, then you will realize that I am he, and that I do

---

[7] Raymond E. Brown, *The Community of the Beloved Disciple: The Life, Loves, and Hates of an Individual Church in New Testament Times* (New York: Paulist Press, 1979), pp. 11-29.

nothing on my own, but I speak these things as the Father instructed me" (John 8:28). The decisive event in Jesus' mission will occur when he is lifted up. Then those who are open will realize that he is "*egō eimi*," that is the one who gave his name to Moses from the burning bush. With this announcement many believed in Jesus. He thereupon professed to them, "You will know the truth and the truth will set you free" (8:32). The truth he had in mind was not a set of ecclesiastical or moral instructions, but that the Father and the Son are one. "So if the Son makes you free, you will be free indeed" (8:36). "If God were your Father, you would love me, for I came from God and now I am here . . . He sent me" (8:42). Jesus was not who they supposed because, "before Abraham was, I am (*egō eimi*)" (8:58). His being lifted up is the greatest sign of all. He is the "*egō eimi*" through whom all things were made.

THE JEWS CRITICAL OF JESUS HEALING THE BLIND MAN (9:1-41)

God often uses human imperfections to his glory, according to the Gospel of John. Jesus, for example, knew that Judas would betray him out of avarice (12:5). But because of that very betrayal Jesus would be lifted up and glorified (13:10-11, 28-31). He healed a blind man (9:3) and raised Lazarus (11:4) to reveal and glorify God. When Jesus restored sight to the blind man onlookers were baffled as to who did it. Jesus had difficulty confirming his identity; so did the blind man (9:9). When the Pharisees ascertained that the blind man had been healed on the Sabbath they immediately charged that Jesus was not from God (9:16) because such action was at cross-purposes with God's intentions for the Sabbath. Some among them argued, however, that only a person from God could perform such signs. When the Jews told the blind man that Jesus was a sinner, the man replied, "One thing I do know, that though I was blind, now I see" (9:25). The blind one who could not see affirmed his belief in the Son of Man (9:38), but the Pharisees who professed to see remained blind in respect to Jesus as Son of God (9:39).

In the long section of John 2–9 perspectives on Jesus found in chapter 1 are reiterated and fleshed out. The chief emphasis is that Jesus is identical with the God who appeared to Moses at the burning bush, was sent from God and is to return to him. His mission in a world that ignores God is to share eternal life through the Holy Spirit. Those who believe are born from above. The signs that point to Jesus' divine origins initiate faith that he is God's Son. The mission of Jesus culminates in his glorification. The glorification occurs according to God's time frame. Jesus' glorification is his being lifted up on the cross, from the tomb, and in his return to God. This is the ultimate sign that Jesus was sent from God.

Jesus showed himself to be from God
because of the sheep God gave him.

Glorification Anticipated and the Disciples Charged

(JOHN 11–17)

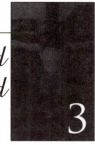

3

Jesus now turns from his major controversies with the Jews to prepare the disciples for their role in the continuing ministry of their glorified and ascended Lord. The signs set forth point ahead to death and resurrection. Jesus' mission includes leaving behind a people, a sheepfold of those who know the shepherd's voice. The disciples will be assisted in this great work through the sending of the Holy Spirit—the *Paraklētos* (Greek).

JESUS THE GOOD SHEPHERD
(10:1-42)

Jesus showed himself to be from God because of the sheep God gave him. "What my Father has given me is greater than all else, and no one can snatch it out of the Father's hand. The Father and I are one" (John 10:29-30). He knew his own sheep and his own knew him (10:14). He is the good shepherd who knows his sheep. Jesus is the true shepherd and his sheep hear his voice and know him (10:3). The sheep will not follow the voice of a stranger (10:5). Those who refuse to believe that Jesus is sent from God are listening to a false shepherd. Only Jesus brings salvation (10:9-10). He was sent from God to lay down his life for the sheep (10:11; 3:16). Not only does Jesus lay down his life for his own people the Jews, but also for others who are not of Israel, thereby foretelling the Gentile mission (10:16; cf. 12:20). Jesus' brothers did not live a goal-oriented life (7:6). All the times in their lives were the same.

Jesus in the Gospel of John was never a victim. Nothing ever happened to him that he did not will. His time of suffering was his moment of glorification. He freely gave his life for the sins of the world. "I lay down my life in order to take it up again" (10:18).

The Jews charged Jesus with equivocating (10:24). Jesus responds that the evidence (signs) all pointed to his Sonship and

35

Messiahship (10:25-29). The Jews took up stones to kill Jesus because, according to them, "You . . . are making yourself to be God" (10:33). Jesus did not deny the charge, but pointed out that his works were the same as God's works (10:37).

THE TIME FRAME OF DEATH, LIFE AND GLORIFICATION (11:1–12:50)

John declared in 1:4 that life came into being from the Word. Jesus is therefore able to give up his own life, then take it up again. He is also able to restore life to the dead. This ability is a decisive witness—a sign that he is from God. His exit from the tomb is his glorification (11:4). The death of Lazarus was not a disaster should Jesus arrive at his tomb. It was an opportunity on the way to Jesus' glorification. The disciples were present at the wedding in Cana. Now a later sign will add to their faith. "For your sake I am glad I was not there, so that you may believe" (11:15).

On the matter of the future of Lazarus Martha exclaimed, "I know that he will rise again in the resurrection on the last day" (11:24). She believed that God on the judgment day would bring the dead to life. Jesus refocused the source of that resurrection. He declared himself the source of life. The resurrection at the end time will occur because of him. "I am the resurrection and the life" (11:25). The one who believes in the Son will never die, that is, will experience only life up until death and again after the judgment, regardless of the interim before the judgment (11:26). Martha confessed a conviction about Jesus congruous with his mission. "Yes, Lord, I believe that you are the Messiah, the Son of God, the one coming into the world" (11:27).

Jesus by his action clearly demonstrated that he was the one through whom all things were made—The Word! Jesus ordered Lazarus who had been dead for four days, "Come out!" (11:43). Lazarus came out, still wrapped in burial cloth. When this news reached the Jewish officials they became alarmed over the popular acclaim for Jesus and grew even more determined to arrange his death. The high priest, Caiaphas, at the demand of certain Pharisees that Jesus must be silenced, uttered a truth far more than he was aware when he said, "It is better for you to have one man die for the people than to have the whole nation destroyed" (11:50). He had in mind that if Jesus rallied the people behind him, Jerusalem could expect retribution from the Romans so that it was better for him to die than that the Romans slaughter numerous Jews. But God intended Caiaphas' declaration as a pronouncement that Jesus would die for the sins of the world. "He prophesied that Jesus was about to die for the nation and not for the nation only, but to gather into one the dispersed children of God" (11:52).

How did Jesus know when his "time" had come? We discover the answer in John 12. An event at the home of Lazarus in Bethany foreshadowed the end. At a dinner with Jesus, Mary poured a pound of pure nard on Jesus' feet and wiped them with her hair (12:3). Judas criticized her action; but Jesus defended her on the grounds that she anticipated his burial. The next day the crowds, as had Nathanael (1:49), declared Jesus "King of Israel" (12:13). Jesus symbolically found a donkey to ride into Jerusalem in the same manner as Solomon when he took over the kingship (1 Kgs. 1:44). The disciples remembered at a later time that these events contributed to his glorification (12:16), that is, the "sign" that he was indeed king of the Jews, the savior of the world.

Jesus made his way to Jerusalem a final time. There he received an unusual request. Some Greeks were in Jerusalem Passover week and having met Philip requested to see Jesus. Philip reported their request to Andrew and they both went to Jesus and told him. Jesus' reaction seems puzzling. "The hour has come for the Son of Man to be glorified" (12:23). What does the request of the Gentiles have to do with the crucial moment of his glorification? We are not told whether the Gentiles ever got to see Jesus. Apparently when the Gentiles requested to see Jesus, he concluded that news regarding the "signs" in respect to his mission had reached both the world of the Jews and the Gentiles, and now his time has arrived. Now his glorification will be of importance to both alike. Jesus' hour is his death (12:24-26). He lived to die—not to die any death, but a death that will draw all people to him, both Jew and Gentile. The disciple likewise must follow him in giving up his or her life in servanthood (12:25).

Jesus prayed to be spared this hour, but he accepted it as the reason for which he came. He was not a victim. He accepted death

as the fulfillment of his mission (12:27). The hour of his glorification was being lifted up. **"And I, when I am lifted up from the
earth, will draw all people to myself"** (12:32). Though Jesus performed many signs among the Pharisees, they did not believe even
as Isaiah had predicted (12:38). Some authorities believed, nevertheless they did not confess for fear they would be put out of the
synagogue. They loved human glory over that which comes from
God, centered upon Jesus (12:43).

In chapters 2–12 all the affirmations about Jesus in John 1 and
13–21 are set forth, and many of them elaborated upon. These are
the signs in words and action that lead to faith. Jesus being lifted up
was the preeminent sign and the implausible climax of his mission.

THE DISCIPLES AS SERVANTS
(JOHN 13:1-38)

In chapter 13 Jesus is eating supper with the disciples. It is
before the Passover (13:1) and Jesus' last meal with the disciples.
Old themes are picked up. Jesus knew he had to depart to the
Father. His time of glorification was near. He loved his disciples to
the end. He modeled servanthood before the disciples. Judas,
however, would betray him.

During the supper Jesus got up, took off his outer robe, tied a
towel around his body, poured water into a basin and commenced
washing the disciples' feet. In that place and time it was not unusual that feet were washed. It was normal at dinners for servants to
wash the feet of the household and its guests. During the day dust
and grime accumulated on bare or sandaled feet. What was different was who it was who washed feet. It was none other than the
one who "had come from God and was going to God" (13:3).

Peter objected when Jesus approached. But Jesus assured him
that unless he washed his feet he would have no share in him. Peter
then acquiesced, saying wash "also my hands and head" (13:9).
Jesus assured him that it was only the feet that needed washing. As
the washing is being discussed the water of baptism comes to mind
as the means through which believers enter into a share with Christ
(3:5). Jesus meets the disciples at the feet, not where life is clean and
orderly, but where it is contaminated with the dust and filth from
many trails and alleys. Jesus meets the sinner where life is the ugli-

est and seamiest. He thereby frees the disciple to meet others at the same place—at the feet. He challenges the disciples. "So if I, your Lord and Teacher, have washed your feet, you also ought to wash one another's feet" (13:14). He sends his disciples out into a corrupted and sinful world to wash feet (13:19).

At the end of chapter 13 Jesus lays out the thoughts he will develop in speaking to the disciples in 14–17. He first mentions that his glorification is already underway (13:31). Second, he reminds the disciples that he is leaving them and they cannot follow (13:33). Third, he gives them a new commandment, "That you love one another. Just as I have loved you, you should also love one another" (13:34). Reference to this commandment will reappear in 1 John (2:7) and 2 John (5). Jesus has now designated the disciples to carry on the ministry he launched. They will emulate his love, just as he emulated the love of the Father. As his ministry comes to an end, theirs will begin (13:35). Finally, Jesus predicted that when he is lifted up the disciples would abandon him.

THE MINISTRY OF THE DISCIPLES
(JOHN 14–17)

In chapter 14 Jesus begins preparing the disciples for the eventuality that, as his ministry winds down, theirs will wind up. When Jesus leaves he will prepare a place for the disciples where he is (14:2). But in John's typical fashion this place seems to have both earthly and heavenly manifestations. The persons the disciples bring to the Lord will have a part in Jesus' preparation, both immediately and at the end time. Thomas expresses puzzlement over where Jesus is going and the way to get there. The place is critical because in it they will share a close relationship with the Father. Jesus focuses on the way to get there. The disciples know the way because they have already embraced that way. "I am the way, and the truth, and the life" (14:6). Those who know Jesus know the Father and possess a role in his house. Philip requests that Jesus show them the Father, but Jesus points to himself, "Whoever has seen me has seen the Father" (14:9; compare 1:18). Jesus once again underscores his departure to the Father. He declares that they will do greater works because he is going to the Father. The love the Son and the Father share will now come to

39

fruition in the disciples. Their love will be multiplied among all those with whom they in turn share that love.

The source of the disciples' greater works will devolve upon the Son, "If in my name you ask me for anything, I will do it" (14:14). Jesus will support the disciples in their ministry. They will be supplied replacement assistance, for Jesus will send another Advocate, the Spirit of Truth (14:16) or the Holy Spirit (14:26). Jesus will not leave them orphaned (14:18). He will come to them; and the Father will come, and they will make their home with them (14:23). The Holy Spirit will likewise abide with and in them (14:17). The disciples of Jesus will be recognized through their keeping of Christ's commandments (14:21, 23; 15:10). When the Advocate or Helper comes he will teach the disciples all things and remind them of everything Jesus said to them (14:25). The ministry which Jesus launched will be fully sustained by the Father, Son, and Spirit when his glorification is complete. If 1 John assists in the interpretation of the Gospel, then it is clear that these promises of the indwelling of the Father, Son and Spirit apply not only to the twelve, but also to all who come to believe that Jesus is the Christ (1 John 2:20-25).

THE MINISTRY AS A VINEYARD

In chapter 10 Jesus employed a corporate metaphor of the shepherd and sheep to describe his relationship with the disciples. In chapter 15 the metaphor is an organic one—the vine and the branches. The Father is involved with the Son in the vineyard. He is the vine grower and the Son is the vine (15:1). The believers are the branches. God prunes the deadwood from the branches so they can produce more fruit. The branches produce fruit because they receive the nourishment that the Father supplies through the Son (15:5). The Father is glorified when the Son is lifted up. He is likewise gloried by those who believe because of the lifted-up Son (15:8). Jesus declares that he is the friend of the believers through his laying down his life for them (15:13-15). He has made known to them everything he has heard from the Father (15:15). Jesus himself selected his disciples (15:16). The world will hate the disciples because the world hated their master, and just as the Son was persecuted so the disciples will be persecuted.

40

THE DISCIPLES AND THE
MISSION OF THE HOLY SPIRIT
(16:1-32)

Chapter 16 focuses on the work and mission of the Holy Spirit commencing with 15:26-27. When the Advocate comes he will testify on Jesus' behalf and the disciples will likewise testify on his behalf. The time will come when the disciples will be put out of the synagogue (16:4). It will be an advantage for Jesus to go away because then the Advocate will come to be with the disciples. The Advocate will prove the world wrong about sin, righteousness and judgment (16:8). Prior to the arrival of the Advocate Jesus came into the world and those who refused to believe were thereby judged (3:18-20; 8:23-26; 12:47-49). The Spirit will lead the disciples into all truth, and glorify Jesus (16:12-14). After Jesus departs the disciples are to ask whatever they desire from the Father and he will give it to them. "Ask and you will receive, so that your joy may be complete" (16:24). Jesus ended by predicting that his disciples would be scattered, perhaps anticipating both the time he was to be lifted up on the cross and also when later persecution set in (16:32, 33).

THE UNITED MINISTRY
(17:1-26)

Chapter 17 contains the famous prayer of Jesus. All these discourses of Jesus, beginning with chapter 13, apparently were given to the disciples at the last meal. Jesus now prayed to the Father highlighting his glorification by the Father. The Father will in turn be glorified by the Son's glorification. God gave the Son the power to share eternal life with those God gave him (17:2). Jesus glorified God by completing the work for which he was sent, and now he calls upon God to give emphasis to the status Jesus possessed prior to his existence in the world (17:5).

Jesus prays for those God has given him. The church of the Lord Jesus Christ is that body for which Jesus prays. He asks the Father to protect those who believe and nurture their oneness even as the Father and Son are one (17:11). He asks the Father not to take them out of the world, but to protect them from the evil one (17:15). Sanctify them in the truth, Jesus declared, because God's word is truth (17:17). They have a mission in the world to emulate the Son who was sent into the world (17:18). Jesus also prayed for those who would believe in Jesus through their word.

The church has its mission in the world to announce the Word given by its Lord. The church is that community which glorifies Christ through announcing his lifting up. By his power and that of the Father and of the Holy Spirit they are in turn lifted up. This oneness in being lifted up, Jesus prays, will enable the world to know that the Father loves the Son and in turn loves those who believe in him (17:23). The end of Christ's mission with and through the disciples is that "the love with which you have loved me may be in them, and I in them" (17:26).

$\mathcal{T}$he $\mathcal{A}$rrest and $\mathcal{J}$ewish $\mathcal{T}$rial of $\mathcal{J}$esus

(JOHN 18:1–27)

We will now take up the chapters in the Gospel of John that comprise the final section—John 18–21. Although these narratives move the "life" of Jesus to its culmination and are independent in that sense, nevertheless they are clearly ensconced in all the earlier affirmations and nuances in the Gospel. Even chapter 21 which some identify as a later addition, may best be understood by considering the trajectories running through chapters 1–20.

THE ARREST
(JOHN 18:1-11)

The Gospel of John makes it clear that Jesus approached his final days with his eyes wide open. The time for his glorification had arrived. He had anticipated these days as early as the wedding in Cana (2:4). He accepted the fact that, though rejected by his own, the chief drawing power to his mission will be his being lifted up. "And I, when I am lifted up from the earth, will draw all people to myself" (John 12:32). He was aware that Judas, one of his disciples with whom he had a close association for some months, would betray him (John 13:21).

Jesus did not perceive himself to be a victim of circumstances. He did not view his situation as an indescribably cruel travesty of justice. Despite Gibson's *The Passion of Christ*, Jesus was not narcissistic in regards to the nuances of his own suffering. Neither, as far as we know, were his torturers sadistic, but certainly cruel. Jesus did not seek to sidestep his mission. He met it head on. He was the one in charge, not the leaders, the military nor the police. He willingly embraced his role as the lamb of God—the sacrifice for the sins of the world (John 1:29).

The discourses of Jesus as he eats his final meal with the disciples are found in chapters 13–17. The meal is now over (18:1).

Judas had earlier left the light of the world to go out into the enveloping darkness (13:30). It is night and in the darkness Jesus makes his way with the disciples across the Kidron valley to a place where there is a garden. In John the place of betrayal is never called Gethsemane, but neither did Matthew (26:36) and Mark (14:32) ever identify Gethsemane as a garden. Gethsemane in Hebrew means an oil press and therefore may have been a garden area of an olive orchard on the Mount of Olives (Mark 14:26). Christians later than the New Testament wrote of the Garden of Gethsemane. Judas had been to the garden with Jesus and the disciples before (18:2). It is possible that Jesus and his disciples spent the nights at Passover time in this garden because it was considered within the required distance for travel.

Judas now brought Roman soldiers together with police from the chief Priests and Pharisees to arrest Jesus. It was dark. They were from the darkness (3:19) and therefore had to furnish their own light (18:3) in order to apprehend the one who is the light of the world (8:12). Keener doubts that Roman soldiers were involved, but the best conclusion seems to be that some Roman soldiers from the Antonio Fortress, along with Jewish temple police accompanied Judas in order to make the arrest.[8] The observation of Hoskyns appears insightful, "In the Johannine account the forces of darkness, the Roman and the Jewish authorities, and the apostate disciple are arrayed against the Christ from the beginning."[9]

As customary in John, Jesus, who knew what was in everyone (2:25), knew why the soldiers had come and what was to happen to him (18:4). As Schnackenburg wrote, "Not for a second does Jesus lose his spiritual superiority, just as, later on, he surrenders neither to physical force (cf. 18:23) nor to threats by the authorities (cf. 19:10f). Even at this hour he shows himself to be the shepherd of those who belong to him, who cares that nothing evil happens to his disciples."[10] Jesus therefore took the initiative. He did not

[8] Keener, Craig S., *The Gospel of John: A Commentary* (Peabody: Hendrickson Publishers, 2003) 2:1078-1080.

[9] E.C. Hoskyns, *The Fourth Gospel*, ed. F.N. Davey (London: Farber & Farber, 1947), p. 509.

[10] Rudolf Schnackenburg, *The Gospel According to St. John* (New York: Crossroad, 1982) 3:225.

wait for the questions of the detachment. Jesus asked them, "Whom are you looking for?" (18:4).

When they asked for Jesus of Nazareth, Jesus declared, *egō eimi*, I am, or it can mean "I am he." Judas stood with those who came in the night, determined to incarcerate the light of the world. When Jesus declared, *"egō eimi"* they fell to the ground. They had no doubt heard the charges of the religious authorities that he claimed divinity and his boldness shocked them (see also John 7:46). It was a numinous experience. Perhaps John suggests that they reacted as if he were the one who appeared to Moses at the burning bush. Jesus made the declaration three times *"egō eimi"* I am (18:5, 6, 7). Ironically, before many hours passed Peter was to deny that he was a disciple of Jesus three times. Jesus affirmed "I am" three times; Peter asserted "I am not" three times. The soldiers, accustomed to being in charge, were not in control. Jesus was in control to the end.

After the second question and response, Jesus requested of the officials that they let the disciples go. Jesus will not have his own endangered. He did not wish to lose a single one (18:9) as he had previously declared (6:39; 10:28; 17:12). "While I was with them, I protected them in your name that you have given me. I guarded them, and not one of them was lost except the one destined to be lost, so that the scripture might be fulfilled" (John 17:12). Jesus is the good shepherd who protects the life of the sheep. "I am the good shepherd. The good shepherd lays down his life for the sheep" (John 10:11).

Peter, threatened by the troops, drew his sword and cut off the right ear of the priest's slave, Malchus. Jesus demanded that Peter put his sword away for he faced his death willingly as a command from the Father (10:17-18). "Am I not to drink the cup that the Father has given me?" Peter was still unclear as to Jesus' mission. In his view Jesus was being victimized. From Jesus' perspective it was rather the detachment of military personnel who were the victims of the circumstances.

THE TRIAL BEFORE ANNAS AND CAIPHAS
(JOHN 18:12-27)

The soldiers therefore bound Jesus and took him to Annas, the father-in-law of Caiphas, the high priest. Annas was the most influential Jewish official at this time even though he was not high priest. He had already served as high priest from AD 6–15. Not only had Caiphas his son-in-law become priest, but also five of his sons served in that capacity. John now calls to mind Caiphas' declaration that it was appropriate for Jesus to die to save the people (11:51-52).[11] By this statement Caiphas set forth the Pharisees' rationale for Jesus' death, and at the same time unintentionally anticipated God's mission to lift up the Son.

In the Gospel of John those who react negatively to Jesus are often simply identified as the Jews. In the Passover days now underway it is the high level Jewish officials who bring the charges. In our current climate the placing of blame for Jesus' death is often overshadowed by charges of anti-Semitism against the authors of the Gospels. Keener has rightly observed,

> In examining this issue from a historical standpoint today, it is important to recall that those who tried Jesus were not the sum total of ethnic Jewry in Jesus' day; there were select members of Jerusalem's municipal aristocracy in league with the high priests and acting to keep peace between Rome and the people. Like most political elites, they gained and held power at the expense of some other people and were resented by various groups they had suppressed or marginalized.[12]

The Gospel writers were no more critical of unbelief among the Jews than the great prophets were of the people of God in earlier centuries. The prophets are sometimes sharp in accusation. Isaiah declared,

> Hear, O heavens, and listen, O earth;
>   for the Lord has spoken:
> I reared children and brought them up,
>   but they have rebelled against me.

---

[11] Keener, pp. 1089-1090.
[12] Ibid., pp. 1084-1085.

The ox knows its owner,
> and the donkey its master's crib;
but Israel does not know,
> my people do not understand.

Ah, sinful nation,
> people laden with iniquity,
offspring who do evil,
> children who deal corruptly,
who have forsaken the Lord,
> who have despised the Holy One of Israel,
> who are utterly estranged! (Isa. 1:2-4).

The charges of Jeremiah were no less pointed,

Therefore once more I accuse you,
> says the Lord,
and I accuse your children's children.
Cross to the coasts of Cyprus and look,
> send to Kedar and examine with care;
> see if there has ever been such a thing.
Has a nation changed its gods,
> even though they are no gods?
But my people have changed their glory
> for something that does not profit.
Be appalled, O heavens, at this,
> be shocked, be utterly desolate,
> says the Lord,
for my people have committed two evils:
> they have forsaken me,
the fountain of living water,
> and dug out cisterns for themselves,
cracked cisterns
> that can hold no water (Jer. 2:9-13).

These charges against the people of God, the descendants of whom are later identified as Jews, are stringent and dramatic. Are Isaiah and Jeremiah anti-Semitic because they are critical of ancient

Semites? Are the Gospel writers anti-Semitic because they indict the leaders of the Jews and several of the people for unbelief? The Gospel writers do not claim, however, as some Christians have assumed, that the Jewish people ethnically have since been forever cursed. According to Matthew the crowd declared, "His blood be on us and our children" (Matt. 27:25). But there is no clue from the text that God indeed accepted and levied that curse. Paul clearly believed that God was not yet through with the Jewish people in that he is still struggling with them in order that they might accept Jesus as Messiah (Rom. 9-11). I must hasten to add, however, that I do not believe that Paul's vision for the future of the Jews provides any insight into the status of the twenty-first century State of Israel.

Many contemporary scholars think that the use of "Jews" in the Gospel of John is tinctured by the fact that in the area of the Johannine churches, the Jewish believers in Christ have been cast out of the synagogue. This separation made a considerable impact on these Messianic Jews now designated as Christians and led to the inclination in the Gospel to lump all Jews together as those opposed to Jesus. Raymond Brown thinks there are four stages through which the churches in the Johannine circle went, (1) the pre-Gospel era, (2) the time during which the Gospel was written, (3) the time at which the Epistles were written reflecting a division among these churches, and (4) the dissolution of the two groups, some into forms of gnosticism, and others into the larger Christian movement.[13] As to the second phase he wrote, "By the time the Gospel was written the Johannine Christians had been expelled from the synagogues (9:22; 16:1) because of what they were claiming about Jesus."[14] Brown dates the main period of the writing of the Gospel as around AD 90. "The expulsion from the synagogues is now past but persecution (16:2-3) continues, and there are deep scars in the Johannine psyche regarding "the Jews."[15] The same scenario is possible if John the Son of Zebedee penned the Gospel in the same time frame.

Much discussion has ensued in the past one hundred years

---

[13] Raymond E. Brown, *The Community of the Beloved Disciple*, pp. 22-24.
[14] Ibid., p. 22.
[15] Ibid., p. 23.

regarding the accuracy of the Gospel reports on the trial of Jesus. It may well have been the case that the authorities didn't fully follow the typical procedures. But even if so, the details seem within the range of historical likelihood. E.P. Sanders, considered one of the current experts on Judaism of the New Testament period, wrote, "The gospel accounts do present problems, but disagreement with the Mishnah is not one of them. . . . The system as the gospel writers describe it corresponds to the system we see in Josephus. The trial of Jesus agrees very well with his stories of how things happened."[16]

The disciples were released from the original arrest (18:8), nevertheless Peter and another disciple followed. A significant question is, who is this "another disciple"[17] (18:15)? O'Day observes that the disciple is not called "the other" disciple, but "another disciple." It is clear from John 20:2-3 that the other disciple and the disciple Jesus loved is one and the same. "So she ran and went to Simon Peter and the other disciple, the one whom Jesus loved, and said to them, "They have taken the Lord out of the tomb, and we do not know where they have laid him." Then Peter and the other disciple set out and went toward the tomb. O'Day therefore concludes that the disciple who gets Peter into the courtyard is another disciple, not the one whom Jesus loved. It would seem that the disciple who got Peter into the courtyard because he knew the high priest lived either in Jerusalem or the environs. Two such disciples were Joseph of Arimathea and Nicodemus (John 19:38-41). Is the "another disciple" one of these two or someone not named?

An ancient understanding is that this "another" disciple (18:15) as well of the other disciple of John 20:2-3 is none other than the disciple whom Jesus loved (19:2) and it is John, one of the twelve and the author of the Gospel. This conclusion, however, seems unlikely.[18] First, why would John the fisherman from Galilee be known, if only casually, by the high priest? Second, if the author

---

[16] E.P. Sanders, *Judaism: Practice and Belief, 63 B.C.E.-66 C.E.* (London: SCM Press, 1992), p. 487.

[17] Gail R. O'Day, "The Gospel of John: Introduction, Commentary, and Reflections," *The New Interpreter's Bible*, ed. Leander Keck (Nashville: Abingdon Press, 1995), p. 808.

[18] Snackenburg, 3:243-245, and Keener, pp. 1090-1091, think the connection is unlikely, but Beasley-Murray considers the evidence strong that the other disciple is the disciple Jesus loved, p. 324.

has in mind mentioning "another disciple" and in that manner referring to the disciple Jesus loved, why does he not make that clear? This whole matter is further complicated by the commonly held view now among critical scholars that John the Son of Zebedee, the Apostle, is not the author of the Gospel. The author may be another John, or the disciple Jesus loved. Beasley-Murray identifies the author as the Evangelist who is neither John the son of Zebedee nor the disciple Jesus loved.[19]

Ben Witherington goes so far as to suggest that the other disciple of 18:15 is indeed the disciple Jesus loved, but that the disciple Jesus loved was not John the son of Zebedee and one of the twelve. Rather, the disciple Jesus loved or the other disciple who goes unnamed made his home in Jerusalem and was not in the circle of the twelve even though he was present at the last meal (John 13:23). He likewise was the author of Epistles of John as well as of the majority of the Gospel (21:24), but not of Revelation, the author of the latter being John the Prophet.[20]

> Sometime in the early 90s, the Beloved Disciple (whose name may have been John, though the text of the Fourth Gospel does not say so) died. In my view, this disciple was not one of the Twelve, but rather, a Judean disciple with close connections to the high priest who lived in Jerusalem and hosted Jesus and the others during Jesus' final Passover. In other words, he was an eyewitness of the Judean parts of Jesus' ministry but not one of the Galilean disciples. After the death of the Beloved Disciple, someone in the Johannine community assembled and edited the memoirs he had written down (See John 21:24; cf. 19:35), probably in the early 90s.[21]

Scholars of the past one hundred years hold various positions in regard to the identity of the author of John. The majority of critical scholars doubt that the author of the Gospel of John is one of

---

[19] Beasley-Murray, p. lxxiv.

[20] Ben Witherington III, *New Testament History: A Narrative Account* (Grand Rapids: Baker Academic, 2001), pp. 396-399.

[21] Witherington, p. 398.

the twelve or more specially, John the brother of James, both of whom are sons of Zebedee. Raymond Brown, who in his commentary affirmed basic Johannine authorship, later joined with other major scholars in denying that the author was John, one of the twelve. Brown published his commentary on John in 1966.[22] In 1982 in his commentary on the Epistles of John, he wrote, "Indeed, I offer no names for the four Johannine figures I posit in the composition of Gjohn and the Epistles, namely, the Beloved Disciple (the source of the tradition about Jesus), the evangelist, the Presbyter (author of the Epistles), and the final redactor of Gjohn."[23] Some scholars hold that the author may be the Elder John of Ephesus mentioned by Eusebius but Brown doubts any connection. "It is useless to press the case that he was John the Presbyter mentioned by Papias [Eusebias, Hist. 3.39.4] or the presbyter of Ephesus who converted Justin Martyr (*Dialogue* 3.1-8.1)."[24] But most critical scholars simply believe that the author cannot be identified with anyone mentioned concretely either in the New Testament or early church history. I think that the Gospel of John is best understood as being for the most part written by John the Son of Zebedee. At the same time I think that the "another" disciple of John (John 18:15) is not the disciple Jesus loved and is a resident of Jerusalem or environs. I think the question of whether John the son of Zebedee is the beloved disciple is a matter open for discussion.

The "another" disciple entered the courtyard since he was known by the high priest, but Peter was not permitted to enter. This disciple then talked with the woman who guarded the gate and arranged for Peter to enter. Jesus has freely admitted his identity all along in John. He is the *egō eimi*, the one who appeared to Moses. He has so declared three times in the process of his arrest (18:5-8). Peter now is going to do the opposite. He is going to declare three times that he is not who he is perceived to be, that is,

[22] Raymond Brown, *The Gospel according to John*, 2 vols. (Garden City, NY: Doubleday, 1966).

[23] Raymond Brown, *The Epistles of John: A New Translation with Introduction and Commentary* (Garden City, NY: Doubleday and Company, 1982), p. 30. As to Brown's reflections on this change see: Brown, *The Community of the Beloved Disciple*, pp. 33-34.

[24] Brown, *The Epistles of John*, op. cit.

one who had been with Jesus.

The role of Peter among the disciples has a different slant in John. Peter is certainly impetuous Peter being the first among the disciples to express and commit himself. In the Synoptics Peter seems to fill an uncontested leadership role. In John he has some competition in this role with the disciple Jesus loved. When Jesus asked the disciples whether they too would leave when many were departing, it was Peter who spoke up, "Lord to whom can we go? You have the words of eternal life" (John 6:68). It was Peter who at first refused to permit Jesus to wash his feet. "Lord, you will never wash my feet" (John 13:7). But he consented to have his feet washed when Jesus announced that Peter then would have no share with him. Peter was the one among the disciples who drew a sword, ready to fight when the police detachments came after Jesus (John 18:10). It was Peter again among the disciples who asserted, "Lord, why can I not follow you now? I will lay down my life for you" (John 13:37). To Peter, Jesus replied, "Will you lay down your life for me? Very truly, I tell you, before the cock crows, you will have denied me three times" (John 13:38). Peter will soon bitterly recognize the fact that he caved in when the officials and the crowds turned against Jesus. The disciple Jesus loved became the exemplary disciple, not Peter, as is indicated by Jesus commending the disciple he loved to the care of his mother (John 19:26-27). After the resurrection Peter continues his role. He was the first to enter the tomb where Jesus was buried and to ascertain that the body was missing (John 20:5-7). In John 21, Peter regains a special status as the one charged with feeding the sheep (John 21:15-19).

Peter's wavering faith now unfolds as he watches from a distance when Jesus was taken into the residence of the high priest. The woman at the gate first asked Peter if he was one of the disciples. He declared, "I am not" (18:17). The slaves and soldiers started a charcoal fire in the courtyard because it was cold, and Peter joined in with these persons in the darkness. (Later, after Peter led the disciples on a fishing trip, they met Jesus on shore and he had a charcoal fire going John 21:9.)

In the meantime Jesus stood before the high priest—Annas—who grilled him about his teaching (18:19, 24). Jesus answered that all his statements were made openly in the synagogues and in the temple, and therefore his instruction can be determined by asking those who listened. If the high priest wished to know what Jesus taught he should have called those who heard him and asked for their input. Jesus wanted to make it clear that he was not involved in a secret conspiracy. He came as a revealer of God's works and words, not as one who divulged secrets in clandestine meetings. "No one has ever seen God. It is God the only Son, who is close to the Father's heart, who has made him known" (John 1:18). Jesus was willing to let his record speak for itself. He resisted giving his views a spin that would be more compatible to the Jewish officials.

An officer, who was convinced that Jesus showed disrespect to the high priest apparently by his refusal to explain himself, questioned Jesus' comportment and struck him on the face. Jesus asked the officer, why, if he had spoken rightly, had the policeman struck him? Schackenburg writes, "For John, Jesus remains, even in his passion, the self-authenticating vessel of revelation, who, at the same time, puts his opponents in the wrong. It is from this point of view also, that Jesus' answer to the servant who strikes him, is formulated."[25]

Annas now sent Jesus on to Caiaphas. Peter showed courage in remaining by the fire. Still he was unwilling to admit that he was a follower of Jesus. The fire of the enemy sustained Peter, not the light provided by the Son of God. "I am the light of the world. Whoever follows me will never walk in darkness but will have the light of life" (John 8:12). The others standing around the fire asked Peter if he was one of the disciples. A second time Peter declared, "I am not" (18:25). But those who stood with Peter would not give up. A relative of the man from whom Peter cut off an ear reported that he had seen Peter in the garden with Jesus. Now dramatically for the third time Peter denied his association with Jesus. At that very moment the cock crowed (18:27)!

Jesus willingly declared his oneness with the God of Abraham, Isaac and Jacob. Peter denied his companionship with Jesus. Raymond Brown wrote, "By making Peter's denials simultaneous with Jesus' defense before Annas, John has constructed a dramatic contrast wherein Jesus stands up to his questioners and denies nothing, while Peter cowers before his questioners and denies everything."[26] Judas betrayed Jesus. Peter did not betray him, but he caved in, in fear and for his own safety. In his persistent denial he turned his back on "I Am", declaring, "I am not!" But Jesus did not give up on Peter and his role in the ongoing mission. "Peter's denials occupy that gray area, marked not by outright betrayal, but by compromise and acquiescence to personal expediency, self-protection, and fear. . . . The Fourth Evangelist thus places before the reader two models of how the faithful can meet adversity and trial: the model of Jesus, who holds nothing back for the sake of those he loves, and the model of Peter, who holds back everything for his own sake."[27]

---

[26] Brown, Raymond, *The Gospel according to John*, 2 vols. (Garden City, NY: Doubleday. 1966) 2:842.

[27] O'Day, pp. 810-811.

The Trial
Before Pilate

(JOHN 18:28–19:16A)

5

By bringing Jesus before Annas and Caiaphas, the Jewish leaders completed their efforts to trip up Jesus. They hoped to present a sure-fire case against him before Pilate. They were dedicated to bringing Jesus to an end. They wanted his death perpetrated according to the rules. They shrewdly sought Pilate's injunction to end Jesus' life by a Roman crucifixion. In that manner they could stay in good graces with the Romans and at the same time shift the responsibility for his death from themselves to the odious Roman overlords. Early in the morning with Jesus in tow they made their way toward Pilate's Jerusalem residence to be first in line as the Roman workday unfolded.

Jesus had already spoken his final words to his disciples and his own people. Now he invites Pilate and whoever among the Romans is listening to consider his mission and his kingdom. The power of his kingship is now announced to those who presume that ultimate power resides in the empire ruled from Rome. Their domain is vast, but finite. Jesus' kingdom is without borders and eternal. Upon the arrival of the Jewish authorities Pilate is patently in charge, but it is Jesus who presides. Schnackenburg observed,

> The "King of the Jews", who is handed over to the possessor of worldly power and who is condemned by him under pressure from the Jewish leaders, is, in reality, the king whose kingdom is not of this world. Even as one mocked and humiliated, he bears the marks of sovereignty and divinity (cf. 19:5-7), and who emerges from the trial the guiltless and justified one as even his judge has to agree with his thrice repeated declaration of innocence.[28]

---

[28] Schnackenburg, 3:241.

The Jewish rules for Passover preparation determined the structure of the subsequent scenes regarding Pilate, the Jewish leaders and Jesus. The leaders brought Jesus to the headquarters, but they themselves would not enter. They remained outside waiting to discuss matters with Pilate on the porch, so they could eat the Passover that night. Keener observed, "Houses of non-Jews were ritually impure; by entering this residence, scrupulous Jews would contact Gentile impurity and hence prove unable to participate fully in the Passover (Num 9:6). Such sensitivities would not have been unusual for the priestly aristocracy, most of whom had *mikvaot* in their own homes. . . ."[29]

As the result, "The Jews, anxiously concerned for their cleanliness, 'so they can eat the passover (lamb), miss the way to the true passover lamb, Christ the fulfillment of their passover feast."[30] Those who perceived themselves to be guardians of the kingdom of God remained outside while the real discussion regarding the kingdom which is not of this world took place inside.

The words and actions of John 18:28 to 19:16 occur in seven scenes outside and inside, outside and inside.[31]

1. (Outside) Jewish authorities demand Jesus' death 18:28-32

2. (Inside) Pilate questions Jesus about his kingship 18:33-38a

3. (Outside) Pilate pronounces Jesus innocent 18:38b-40

4. (Inside) The Soldiers scourge Jesus 19:1-3

5. (Outside) Pilate again pronounces Jesus innocent 19:4-7

6. (Inside) Pilate questions Jesus about his origin 19:8-11

7. (Outside) Pilate hands Jesus over for execution 19:12-16

---

[29] Keener, p. 1099.
[30] Schnackenburg, 3:244.
[31] So Schnackenburg (3:242) and Culpepper.

1. (OUTSIDE) JEWISH AUTHORITIES DEMAND JESUS' DEATH (18:28-32)

In order to converse with the leaders who refused to come inside, Pilate went outside and asked what charges the Jews wished to press against Jesus. Since Roman soldiers had been involved in arresting Jesus, he apparently already knew that they wished to accuse him of some crime. Pilate now seeks out their official allegation. The Jewish leaders declared Jesus a criminal without specifying his offense. Since their charge was so generic Pilate proposed that the conviction of Jesus was more properly a matter of local Jewish jurisdiction and that they should judge him themselves (18:31). They, however, became more explicit. They demanded that Pilate order an end of Jesus' life by crucifixion. They pressed the matter further by pointing out that while they could judge Jesus they had no authority to put him to death.

The reader is reminded that Jesus designated his death as a lifting up, that is, being crucified for whatever the alleged infractions (18:32). It was neither the Jewish leaders nor the Roman governor who determined Jesus' death by crucifixion, but God and his Son. "The chief priests clearly wished to ensure that Jesus was not viewed as a martyr for God's cause, but as an imposter who died under the curse of God. By contrast the Evangelist sees in the death of Jesus by crucifixion God's way of fulfilling his purpose to 'lift' up Jesus in the glory of divine love to enthronement with himself; thereby the saving sovereignty is opened for all the world, and the exalted Lord can draw all who will into the eternal life of the kingdom of God."[32]

John supplies no information about Pilate, not even that he was the Roman governor of the region. He assumes that his readers are sufficiently informed as to his position. Pilate served as the fifth governor of the province of Judea from AD 26 to 37. He therefore had been governor for at least four years before his confrontation with Jesus. He had no doubt heard something of the stir Jesus created in Galilee and Jerusalem even if he took little or no inter-

---

[32] Beasley-Murray, p. 328.

est. Pilate was most likely of an upper class or equestrian Roman family. His responsibilities in the province of Judea were to maintain law and order, adjudicate major legal cases and collect taxes. Governmental decisions in regard to routine matters largely revolved upon the Jewish High Priest and the aristocracy or Sanhedrin in Jerusalem.

A lengthy statement by Philo (20 BC–AD 50) sheds light upon Pilate's personal characteristics and his relationships with the Jews. Philo's discourse including comments on Pilate was presented at Rome in AD 40.

Pilate was an official who had been appointed procurator of Judaea. With the intention of annoying the Jews rather than of honouring Tiberius, he set up gilded shields in Herod's palace in the Holy City. They bore no figure and nothing else that was forbidden, but only the briefest possible inscription, which stated two things—the name of the dedicator and that of the person in whose honour the dedication was made. But when the Jews at large learnt of this action, which was indeed already widely known, they chose as their spokesmen the king's four sons, who enjoyed prestige and rank equal to that of kings, his other descendants, and their own officials, and besought Pilate to undo his innovation in the shape of the shields, and not to violate their native customs, which had hitherto been invariably preserved inviolate by kings and emperors alike. When Pilate, who was a man of inflexible, stubborn and cruel disposition, obstinately refused, they shouted, "Do not cause a revolt! Do not cause a war! Do not break the peace! Disrespect done to our ancient laws brings no honour to the Emperor. Do not make Tiberius an excuse for insulting our nation. He does not want any of our traditions done away with. If you say that he does, show us some decree or letter or something of the sort, so that we may cease troubling you and appeal to our master by means of an embassy". This last remark exasperated Pilate most of all, for he was afraid that if they really sent an embassy, they would bring accusations against the rest of his administration as well, specifying in detail his venality, his violence, his thefts, his assaults, his abusive behaviour, his frequent executions of untried prisoners, and his endless savage ferocity. So, as he was a spiteful and angry person, he was in a serious dilemma; for he had neither the courage to remove what he had once set up, nor the desire to do anything which would please his subjects, but at the same time he was well aware of Tiberius' firmness on these matters. When the Jewish officials saw this, and realized that Pilate was regretting what he had done, although he did not wish to show it, they wrote a letter to Tiberius, pleading their case as forcibly as they could. What words, what threats Tiberius uttered against Pilate when he read it! It would be superfluous to describe his anger, although he was not easily moved to anger, since his reaction speaks for itself. For immediately, without even waiting until the next day, he wrote to Pilate, reproaching and rebuking him a thousand times for his new-fangled audacity and telling him to remove the shields at once and have them taken from the capital to the coastal city of Caesarea (the city named Sebaste after your great-grandfather), to be dedicated in the temple of Augustus. This was duly done. In this way both the honour of the emperor and the traditional policy regarding Jerusalem were alike preserved.[33]

Pilate pursued his own interests and ends, but always with a wary eye toward Rome, well aware of the need to be perceived as a governor loyal to the emperor.

2. (INSIDE)
PILATE QUESTIONS JESUS
ABOUT HIS KINGSHIP
(18:33-38A)

Pilate must have considered Jesus more than a common criminal, perhaps anticipating, because of conversations with the

---

[33] Philo, *Legatio* 299-305, translated by E.M. Smallwood, *Philonis Alexandini Legatio ad Gaium* (Leiden: E.J. Brill, 1970).

Jewish leaders, that he aspired to political power. Seeking to get to the bottom of the matter Pilate turned from the leaders and reentered the royal residence so he could interrogate Jesus. Wasting no time he put the question bluntly, "Are you the King of the Jews?" (18:33). In John's Gospel "king of Israel" was first employed by Nathanael (John 1:49). Jesus persistently sought to avoid a royal title before the time of his glorification (John 6:15). The people, however, declared him king of Israel as he entered Jerusalem, without Jesus' objection (12:13).

Now Pilate asks Jesus if political hegemony is what the Jewish preoccupation with him is all about. The Jewish leaders at the first appearance of Pilate on his portico did not allege any political claims by Jesus. The scenario is similar to that in Mark. The demons openly declare that Jesus is the Holy one of God (Mark 1:24), but no human recognized his status until considerably later. The religious leaders refused to recognize anything divine in the words and works of Jesus. They are the dense ones. Several persons in John's Gospel anticipate Jesus as the coming king from early in his ministry. Pilate now presses Jesus for the reason, if not on political grounds, why the Pharisees are out to eliminate him.

Jesus asked Pilate why he inquired about his kingship suggesting that Pilate must have heard of such charges (18:34). Pilate clearly conducted the interrogation as if he were the one in control, not Jesus. He essentially ignores Jesus' question and professes to know little and care less about Jewish affairs (18:35). Nevertheless, he does need to know why the Jewish officials arrested Jesus. Pilate therefore inquires again, this time with a more open-ended question, "What have you done?" (18:35). Jesus instead reverts to Pilate's question about kingship indicating that he will respond to Pilate on his own terms.

Jesus did not deny kingship, but professed dominion in a realm of a different sort. He did not speak of himself, but of his kingdom, that is, his kingly rule. "Jesus answered, 'My kingdom is not from this world. If my kingdom were from this world, my followers would be fighting to keep me from being handed over to the Jews. But as it is, my kingdom is not from here'" (John 18:36). Jesus' announced kingdom is not of this world. Were it from this world his disciples would be trained in resistance (18:36). Brown's comment is appropriate. "Jesus does not deny that his kingdom or kingship affects this world, for the world will be conquered by those who believe in him (1 John 5:4). But he denies that his kingdom belongs to this world; *like himself, it comes from above.*"[34] Jesus now openly professes to be a king but of his own devising, that is, by, from and of another realm. "For this I was born, and for this I came into the world, to testify to the truth. Everyone who belongs to the truth listens to my voice" (18:37).

Jesus returned at this point to claims that surfaced earlier. The difference between those who are in on the truth and those who are not is that those who know the truth listen to Jesus. "But because I tell the truth, you do not believe me. Which of you convicts me of sin? If I tell the truth, why do you not believe me? Whoever is from God hears the words of God. The reason you do not hear them is that you are not from God" (John 8:45-47). "The gatekeeper opens the gate for him, and the sheep hear his voice. He calls his own sheep by name and leads them out" (John 10:3). "My sheep hear my voice. I know them, and they follow me. I give them eternal life, and they will never perish" (John 10:27-28). The truth is all tied up with who Jesus is and what he teaches.

Pilate responded with the proverbial "What is truth?" Pilate most likely was not expressing epistemological skepticism in regard to ascertaining truth. Probably he was professing uncertainly as to whether he could get at the bottom of why the Jews wanted so desperately to execute Jesus. He probably also perceived the signals coming from Jesus himself as mixed. Jesus obviously didn't come off as a counter revolutionary against the Roman government. Neither did he appear to be a common criminal. He exhibited no typical political aspirations. Pilate's rejection of Jesus' response was neither philosophical skepticism nor irony. It was a rejection of Jesus himself and his kingdom. According to John, Pilate pushed aside the claims of Jesus without serious consideration. He had little desire to hear Jesus out. He rejected whatever case Jesus might present with only lingering curiosity over its possible facticity (see 19:8-12).[35]

---

[34] Brown, p. 869.
[35] Schnackenburg, 3:251.

Jesus located the truth, not in a philosopher's ontological propositions, or in the issues of a religious debater, but in himself. He expressed little interest in multifold ecclesiastical pronouncements. He declared, "I am the way, the truth and the life" (John 8:32). The truth was all tied up in the declaration that he came from God and was returning to God (John 14:6 as first declared in 1:17). "Manifestly, Jesus is not speaking of truth in an abstract, or even general way, but specifically in relation to his ministry. He came among men with a mission from God to bear witness to the truth of God's saving sovereignty, and to reveal it in word and deed."[36]

3. (OUTSIDE) PILATE PRONOUNCES JESUS INNOCENT (18:38B-40)

Pilate, after his interview with Jesus, returned to the courtyard and asserted to the Jews, "I find no case against him" (18:38). What does Pilate mean that he finds no case against Jesus? My presumption is that he means that he has not discovered any threat to Rome in Jesus' disposition and teachings. Pilate based this decision on political, not theological concerns. I suspect too, that he identified no religious grounds for crucifying Jesus. Most Romans of the time, except for certain philosophers, were polytheistic. Adding a newly announced deity was never a problem.

Furthermore, religious people in Rome and Greece believed that gods had territorial franchises. Zeus held sway over the Grecian lands and it was appropriate to pay deference to him when in Corinth. Jupiter ruled Italy so that respect for him should occupy the Romans. Pilate no doubt believed that it was fully appropriate for Jews to worship Yahweh in Jerusalem and for others to pay him deference while there. On the other hand he assumed the privilege of worshiping the appropriate Roman deities in Caesarea where he resided most of the year. As governor he was not charged with refereeing religious beliefs and practices, only crises that impacted the hegemony of Rome. He himself may not have been very religious though the impact of his wife's dream as reported in

---

[36] Beasley-Murray, pp. 331-332.

Matthew (27:19) suggests that she had religious convictions.

Pilate most likely heard that the Jewish leaders condemned Jesus on the ground that he claimed kingship. Kingship and Messiahship were perceived to be one and the same. Pilate may not have realized how intent the Jewish leaders were in rejecting any claims Jesus might make in respect to being sent from God. In Roman popular religion messengers were regularly sent from the deities (Acts 14:12). At the same time Pilate did not want to dismiss Jewish concerns, for he wanted it to be clear that he was in charge. Perhaps in irony and also to needle, Pilate asked the Jews gathered before the residence if they wanted him to release the "King of the Jews" in anticipation of the Passover. He knew that declaring Jesus king was a slap in their face. But he felt no pressure to kowtow to Jewish predilections. They were in no position to countermand Pilate's sarcasm. Instead of agreeing to set Jesus free they demanded the release of Barabbas, who in contrast with Jesus was a known felon, or more specifically a robber. In Mark, Barabbas is charged with having committed murder during an insurrection (15:7). He was therefore connected with some sort of political uprising and an obvious liability from the perspective of Rome. By rules regarding a release at Passover time, it was the Jewish leaders' call. Because of their demand to release Barabbas, Pilate was unable to unencumber himself of responsibilities regarding Jesus as easily as he wished. What to do with Jesus had become even more complicated rather than less so as Pilate had hoped.

4. (INSIDE)
THE SOLDIERS SCOURGE JESUS
(19:1-3)

Pilate, feeling it imperative to placate the Jews, returned inside and had Jesus flogged (19:1). The showpiece of the atrocities against Jesus in Mel Gibson's *The Passion of the Christ* was the flogging even superseding Jesus' excruciating death on the cross. John provides no insights into the suffering involved in flogging, probably because many persons in the ancient world had witnessed the mutilation of the flesh and the attendant harrowing pain. According to Beasley-Murray, flogging "As administered by Romans it could be one of three kinds: the *fustigatio*, a beating of less severe kind, *flagellatio*, a flogging, or *verberatio*, a scourging, which was the most terrible of all and was always associated with other punishments, including crucifixion.[37] It is Beasley-Murray's view, based on the work of Blinzler, that Jesus received the most severe scourging. It is difficult to know, I think, based upon the information in John or the other Gospels, exactly which flogging took place.[38]

It is clear that Gibson depicted the flogging according to the most severe form. Blinzler described scourging,

> The delinquent was stripped, bound to a post or a pillar, or sometimes simply thrown on the ground, and beaten by a number of torturers until the latter grew tired and the flesh of the delinquent hung in bleeding shreds. In the provinces this was the task of soldiers. Three different kinds of implements were customary. Rods were used on freemen; military punishments were inflicted with sticks, but for slaves scourges or whips were used, the leather thongs of these being often fitted with a spike or with several pieces of bone or lead joined to form a chain. The scourging of Jesus was carried out with these last named instruments.[39]

Beasley-Murray believes that this most severe scourging may be corroborated by fact of Jesus' premature death. "It is generally believed that the suffering of this severe scourging was the reason why Jesus was unable to carry his cross all the way to his execution, and why he died so soon after being crucified."[40]

Whatever the case, John omits explicit details in respect to the scourging. Apparently it is of greater interest to him to depict Pilate, the epitome of worldly power, as moving ahead, confident of his decisions. But in point of fact Pilate has permitted the situation to

---

[37] Beasley-Murray, p. 335.
[38] For uncertainty regarding the type of flogging see Keener who thinks that contemporary readers would not have been aware of these distinctions, pp. 1118-1120.
[39] Beasley-Murray, pp. 335-336. The quote is from J. Blintzler, *Der Prozess Jesu* (Regensburg:Velag Pustet, 1969), pp. 321-322.
[40] Beasley-Murray, p. 336.

get out of hand. It is only Jesus whose kingdom is not of this world who remains in control throughout these momentous hours.

The soldiers compounded the abuse of Jesus initiated by Pilate through ridicule. They placed a crown of thorns on his head and a kingly robe on his body. The crown according to Keener, ". . . was probably an instrument of mockery rather than one of torture."[41] Most scholars believe the crown was constructed from the great thorns of the date palm which were readily available and looked more like an Indian's headdress. Gibson's movie depicts it as drawing blood. The soldiers paraded before him with taunts, "Hail, King of the Jews" (19:3). Then they struck him on the face to indicate that they had no fear of retaliation from deity, even though earlier, upon first seeing him they or their fellows dropped to the ground in numinous caution. The fact that Jesus appeared helpless before Pilate incited their bravado. Even while undergoing ridicule and bodily torture, Jesus stays the course and stands above the fray.

5. (OUTSIDE) PILATE AGAIN PRONOUNCES JESUS INNOCENT (19:4-7)

Pilate returned to the Jews outside and told them that he found no case against Jesus. He apparently approved the raillery of the soldiers for he did not instruct them to remove the kingly parody. Pilate now displays Jesus in his ridiculous and emaciated physiognomy for their approval. It is his hope that they will acquiesce to release him. Pilate, with dramatic flair, presented Jesus, famous in the King James translation, "Behold the man! (John 19:5), in the Latin, "Ecce Homo." (The NRSV and the NIV translate the phrase "Here is the man!")

Bultmann has captured what I think is the intent of both Pilate and of John,

Clearly the purpose in this is to make the person of Jesus appear to the Jews as ridiculous and harmless, so that they should drop their accusations. Hence Jesus has to step

[41] Keener, p. 1122.

forth as the caricature of a king, and Pilate presents him with the words, "That is the man! Look at the pitiful figure!" But to the mind of the Evangelist the entire paradox of the claim of Jesus is in this way fashioned into a tremendous picture. The very truth it is just such a man who asserts that he is the king of truth! The declaration . . . ("The Word became flesh") has become visible in its extremest consequence.[42]

The decision of the Jews to kill Jesus is now transparent and whatever Pilate does in no way appeases them. Upon the presentation of Jesus the chief priests and temple police were even more determined. They cried out, "Crucify him! Crucify him!" Pilate still insisted, however, that if they wanted Jesus killed they should do it themselves (19:6). The Jewish leaders realizing that it was not easy to sway Pilate's conviction that Jesus was harmless and innocent of common crimes finally announced a more specific charge "He has claimed to be Son of God." That put the matter in a different light. What if Jesus was indeed one of the many deities that on occasion appeared to humans according to the ancient poets of Rome and Greece? The declaration disturbed Pilate to the extent that he went back inside to confront Jesus. Whatever Pilate made of the charge it was a clear ground for the death sentence according to the manner in which the Jewish leaders interpreted the Law of Moses (Lev. 24:16). "The messianic pretension was serious enough, but the claim to be Son of God, with its accompanying roles of Redeemer and Revealer was intolerable. It remains the great stumblingblock to Israel to this day."[43]

6. (INSIDE) PILATE QUESTIONS JESUS ABOUT HIS ORIGIN (19:8-11)

"Now when Pilate heard this, he was more afraid than ever" (19:8). Just perhaps Jesus was more than he had imagined! Pilate

---

[42] Rudolf Bultmann, *The Gospel of John* (Oxford: Blackwell, 1971), p. 659.
[43] Beasley-Murray, p. 339.

asked Jesus bluntly, "Where are you from?" (19:9). This time Jesus did not answer. Jesus had already declared that he had come into the world to establish a kingdom not from this world (18:36-38). What more can he say to convince this hardened soldier-politician? "As a Roman, he would have known many stories of deities appearing in human form and of judgment coming on mortals who rejected them. Naturally, a polytheist would be more open to multiple claims of divine sonship than a monotheist, but on the level of Johannine theology as a whole, this feature of the account likewise exudes irony: the agent of Rome proves more ready to believe something divine about God's son than his own people do (cf. 1:11; Mark 15:39).[44]

Pilate chided Jesus over his refusal to speak (19:10). He pointed out that he could release Jesus or have him crucified. Jesus maintained control over the situation just as he had in the garden where he wasn't overpowered by the soldiers, but went with them willingly. Now Jesus makes clear to Pilate that the outcome is in God's hands not those of Pilate. "You would have no power over me unless it had been given you from above" (19:10). So, indirectly Jesus declared himself to be the Son of God! "With these words, Pilate, who subjects Jesus to his supposed power, becomes the one subject, and Jesus, the seemingly powerless one, shows himself to be the one who is free and possesses power."[45] Pilate "from then on" tried to release Jesus, but the Jews were insistent. In this manner they unwittingly complied with God's will that Jesus be lifted up. O'Day wrote, "At the end of the trial, when Jesus is handed over to be crucified, Pilate and the Jewish religious leaders think that the moment of judgment on Jesus has arrived, that his 'kingship' has come to an end. Yet it is not the moment of Jesus' judgment, but theirs. Nor is it the end of Jesus' kingship, but the prelude to his exaltation and final 'enthronement' on the cross (19:17-22)."[46] Finally in desperation over Pilate's reluctance, the Jews are willing to go so far as to charge that Jesus proclaimed himself a king; a treason, they reminded Pilate, against Rome!

[44] Keener, p. 1125.
[45] Schnackenburg, 3:261.
[46] O'Day, p. 827.

67

7. (OUTSIDE) PILATE HANDS JESUS OVER FOR EXECUTION (19:12-16)

Pilate, finally deciding that he could not placate the determination of the Jewish leaders, brought Jesus outside and sat on the judgment seat. It was the day of preparation for the Sabbath. Reflecting on the implications of the time of day for John, Schnackenburg wrote, "For him, Jesus is undoubtedly the NT passover lamb, of whom 'not a bone' was 'broken' (19:36, cf. on 18:38). He could likewise have connected the 'sixth hour' with this. It was the hour at which, in those days, preparation was made for the slaughtering of the passover lambs in the temple."[47]

Once again Pilate announced what Jesus embraced, "Here is your King" (19:15). The God-designated king came into the world and his own received him not (1:11). They adamantly cried out, "Crucify him!" (19:15). To redirect the kingly designation the Jews responded, "We have no king but the emperor" (19:15). Pilate finally gave in and turned Jesus over to be crucified. "The reminder of the emperor is enough to break down the last resistance of Pilate; he cannot and will not risk the threatened report to his chief superior (cf. v. 12). He too sacrifices his conviction, the knowledge of the accused's innocence, to his personal ambition, to his concern for rank and well-being."[48]

---

[47] Schnackenburg, 3:265.
[48] Ibid., 266.

The Lifting Up and Taking Down to be Lifted Up Again

6

(JOHN 19:16B-42)

The depiction of Jesus' crucifixion in John moves swiftly. The detail is minimal in respect to the how the retinue arrived at the site, the taunting of the mobs along the way, the attachment of Jesus' hands and legs to the cross, the excruciating pain from the nails, the height of the cross, the incessant thirst, or Jesus' precipitate demise. For details of this sort one must depend upon the later dramatic visionaries who inspired Gibson's *The Passion of the Christ*. The details supplied by John are, however, poignant for theological reflection. "The Fourth Evangelist takes traditional material about Jesus' death and shapes it to fit his understanding of Jesus' death as the hour at which he completes God's work (19:30)."[49] We will reflect on seven aspects of these last moments in the life of the savior.

1. The crucifixion (19:15b-18)

2. The inscription (19:19-22)

3. The seamless tunic (19:23-24)

4. Jesus' mother and the beloved disciple (19:25-27)

5. Jesus' last words (19:28-30)

6. The piercing of Jesus' side (19:31-37)

7. The burial (19:38-42)

---

[49] O'Day, p. 829.

1. THE CRUCIFIXION
(19:15B-18)

Pilate turned Jesus over the Roman soldiers to carry out the crucifixion (19:16, 23). Jesus carried his cross to the place of the skull called Golgotha. What he carried was the crossbeam, not the upright, the two being attached together at the site.[50] Jesus himself alone bore the weight of the beam for the sins of the world. The report of the Synoptics that Simon of Cyrene was pressed into service to carry the cross for Jesus gives emphasis to his weakness and loss of blood following upon his scourging.

Executioners usually tied victims to the cross with ropes but in some cases hastened their death by also nailing their wrists (20:25). The nails were typically five to seven inches long, enough to penetrate both the wrist and well into the wood of the cross. One being executed on the cross could not swat flies from one's wounds nor withold one's bodily wastes from coming out while hanging naked for hours and sometimes days. The upright stakes were normally ten feet at the highest, more often closer to six or seven feet so that the man hung barely above the ground, with a seat (sedile) in the middle; animals sometimes assaulted the feet of the crucified. Romans could employ high crosses to increase visibility for significant public executions (Suetonius Galba 9.1), and given the use of the branch hyssop here (19:29; cf. Mark 15:36), Jesus may have been slightly higher than usual.[51]

Jesus was crucified with two criminals, one on each side, but John gives no information about them. The focus is on Jesus.

2. THE INSCRIPTION
(19:19-22)

Pilate's ironic declaration, "The King of the Jews" was affixed to the cross for all to see. Jesus' mission has reached the initial

---

[50] Keener, p. 1134.
[51] Ibid., p. 1136.

stages of its completion. He has been lifted up. As we have pointed out previously his being lifted up is the goal of his ministry. The word lifted up in the Greek *hypso* has a double meaning. It can mean a physical lifting up. It can also mean exaltation. For John, when Jesus was lifted up on the cross he was also exalted. This was his moment of glory (12:23). O'Day wrote, "The overlap of crucifixion and exaltation conveyed by [John 3:14] is crucial to Johannnine soteriology, because the Fourth Evangelist understands Jesus' crucifixion, resurrection, and ascension as one continuous event. Verse 14 also contains a key to the theological ground of the Evangelist's attraction to irony; the cross as humiliation is actually exaltation."[52]

Pilate inscribed the true role of Jesus at the very place where Jesus is lifted up. "Jesus of Nazareth, the King of the Jews" (19:19). The inscription was written in Hebrew, in Latin, and in Greek. The sign announced that Jesus was king over all who spoke those languages. But he was king not just for them, but for the whole world. "For God so loved the world that he gave his only Son, so that everyone who believes in him may not perish but may have eternal life" (John 3:16). "The three languages are to announce Jesus' kingship officially to the whole world."[53] Pilate, who plays politics to the end, in order to placate the Jews, but also to taunt them, inadvertently announced who it was exposed on the cross. Jesus was on the cross, not as a victim, but as one who freely gave his life in order to take away the sins of the world (1:29) and "to gather into one the dispersed children of God" (11:52). As O'Day wrote, "The death of Jesus is not the tragedy for the Fourth Evangelist; 'the Jews" loss of their relationship with God is."[54] The Jews tried to get Pilate to revise the inscription so as to declare that Jesus rather claimed to be king of the Jews. But Pilate refused to get sidetracked from his desire to place the blame for Jesus' death squarely upon the shoulders of the Jews. Pilate, declared defiantly "What I have written, I have written."

---

[52] O'Day, p. 552.
[53] Schnackenburg, 3:272.
[54] O'Day, p. 825.

3. THE SEAMLESS TUNIC
(19:23-24)

The soldiers are insensitive and fearless, yet they followed the customs in respect to the death of any other criminal. They divided up his clothes among themselves. When they came to his tunic they found that it was seamless. Rather than divide it into sections they decided to preserve it intact so they cast lots for it. Even their shameful action, however, was God decreed, as declared in the Psalms (19:24). The seamless garment may imply the garment of a priest (Lev. 21:10), or it may signify the unity of the church. However, since the soldiers took away Jesus' tunic, perhaps of more importance is that it is no longer in the possession of Jesus. When Jesus washed the disciples' feet he put his robe aside so as to serve. In Jesus' triumphal act on the cross in which he took away the sins of the world, his tunic was likewise laid aside.

In the final analysis though Pilate and the soldiers perceived themselves to be in charge, Jesus determined the details of his death even until the end, even to the extent of fulfilling Scriptures. "For this reason the Father loves me, because I lay down my life in order to take it up again. No one takes it from me, but I lay it down of my own accord" (10:17-18). The soldiers divided Jesus' clothes into four parts, one for each soldier. Since a seamless tunic was prized and more expensive they decided to cast lots for it. The casting of lots John declared fulfilled the affirmation in Psalm 22:18 regarding the dividing of the garments. The soldiers likely had dice so as to pass the time of day as they guarded the grounds of crucifixion. They wiled away the hours while the one on the cross gave his life for their counterparts across the ages.

4. JESUS' MOTHER AND
THE BELOVED DISCIPLE
(19:25-27)

Four soldiers carried out their guard duties in the vicinity of the three crosses. Four women who had been impressed by Jesus' mission looked on from a distance. They were his mother and her sister, Mary the wife of Clopas and Mary Magdalene. The concern of Jesus on the cross was not over his shameful end, for indeed it was his glory (12:23). Neither was he self absorbed with the excruciating pain. Rather, he was focused upon the greater works that were to transpire in the loving community created by his disciples (14:12). The loving community of his followers was the focus of his extended prayer at the end (17:20-24).

Mary the mother of Jesus in John is only mentioned prior to the cross scene at the wedding in Cana (2:1-2). But she is part of the new family that will carry on Jesus' ministry. Jesus announced to her that she should now consider John her son (19:26). John in turn should consider her his mother and take care of her. O'Day believes it ". . . is possible to interpret Jesus' mother as representing the sweep of Jesus' incarnate ministry from beginning to end, and the beloved disciple as representing those for whom Jesus gives his life in love at his hour and who are commanded to love in the same way."[55] The death of Jesus is the link between the past of Jesus' work and its future. The kingdom not of this world is focused upon caring and feeding (21:15ff). Earlier when Mary requested Jesus' help, he told her his hour was not yet come, though he went ahead and changed water to wine (2:4). Now that his hour has arrived he makes arrangements for her future care. The concern of one believer for one another in the new community of faith is to be even stronger than the normal familial bonds (14:18-21).

5. JESUS' LAST WORDS
(19:28-30)

From the Gospel of John we know little about the physical aspects of Jesus' death. We know that he thirsted thereby affirming his humanity. But the thirst is not depicted as debilitating. A jar of sour wine stood nearby and someone standing there filled a sponge, put it on the end of a stick, and held it up to Jesus' mouth. After he received the wine Jesus exclaimed, "it is finished." John declared that Jesus' thirst was a fulfillment of Scripture, referring to Psalm 22:15; 69:21. Jesus bowed his head and gave up his spirit. He was in charge, even of his death. He did not linger. His mission has reached its climactic peak. "Jesus' death is not a moment of defeat or despair . . . but a moment of confidence in his completion

[55] O'Day, p. 832.
[56] Ibid., p. 833.

of God's work in the world (17:4). Jesus' death on the cross is the final expression of his love for his own (cf. 13:1; 15:13) and his love for God (14:30-31)."[56]

The recent interest in Jesus' death has been transfixed on Mel Gibson's, *The Passion of the Christ*. Jesus' death is graphically presented with close-up depictions of the pain, blood, and the final excruciating expiration. Several have reported their newly gained respect for Christ and his sacrificial death through seeing the film. Whatever the merits of watching Gibson's film, it is clear that John has almost no interest in dwelling upon Christ's anguish. He focuses instead upon how God is glorified when Jesus is lifted up! He also dwells on the new community of love empowered by the Holy Spirit that results. "For God so loved the world that he gave his only Son, so that everyone who believes in him may not perish but may have eternal life" (3:16). What will draw all men to God is neither the quantity of blood nor the grievousness of the suffering. It is the love radiating from the one lifted up!

Justo L. González, the church historian, wrote regarding the memory of Jesus in the early church, "Those early communion services did not center on the Lord's passion, but rather on his victory by which the new age had dawned. It was much later—centuries later—that the focus of Christian worship shifted towards the death of Jesus."[57] For John, Jesus' death was his glory, and his resurrection the beginning of his return to the Father. John was not engrossed as later Christians over the wretchedness of Christ's final hours. Even the well-known Protestant hymn, "When my Love to Christ Grows Weak," centers upon Christ's suffering rather than the glory of his elevation to the cross and his unanticipated resurrection.

> When my love to Christ grows weak, When for deeper faith I seek,
> Then in tho't I go to Thee, Garden of Gethsemane!

---

[56] Ibid., p. 833.

[57] Justo L. González, *The Story of Christianity* (San Francisco: HarperCollins, 1984), p. 20.

There I walk amid the shades, While the ling'ring twilight fades,
See that suff'ring, friendless One, Weeping, praying there alone.

When my love for man grows weak, When for Stronger faith I seek
Hill of Calvary! I go To the scenes of fear and woe.

There behold His agony, Suffered on the bitter tree;
See His anguish, see His faith Love triumphant still in death.

Then to life I turn again, Learning all the worth of pain,
Learning all the might that lies in a full self-sacrifice.

Another hymn, "In the Cross of Christ I glory," captures more the focus of John's view of events leading up to Jesus upon the cross.

6. THE PIERCING OF JESUS' SIDE
(19:31-37)

The Jews, in anticipation of the Sabbath, wanted those on the cross removed before the sunset hour so they sought permission from Pilate to hasten the death of the three by breaking their legs. A person might linger on the cross for some days before dying, but not with broken legs. When the soldiers came to Jesus, however, he was already dead, so they didn't break his legs. Perhaps, as some suggest, this was because of his emaciating scourging. A soldier pierced his side and blood and water flowed out (19:34). John declared that the Scripture had foretold in advance that no bones would be broken (Exod. 12:36; Ps. 34:20), but he would be pierced (Zech. 12:10). The details of Jesus' death, even as to time, were God determined and orchestrated. Neither Pilate nor the Jewish leaders initiated on their own accord the body piercing.

The significance of the blood and water make clear that Jesus was indeed human. "And the Word became flesh and lived among us" (1:14). As the Hebrews writer put it, "Since therefore, the children share flesh and blood, he himself likewise shared the same things. . . ." (Heb. 2:14). But statements in John often have more than one level of meaning. John may at this point pick up on the previously announced sacrifice of the Lamb of God (1:29) and the manner in which salvation is apprehended through his blood sacrifice (6:54) and through the water of baptism (3:5). Now that these events have occurred John declares that one who witnessed these final hours testified as to their veracity and his testimony is true (19:35). The disciple Jesus loved stood among the women and it is no doubt him that John has in mind. The truthfulness of his witness is again affirmed in 21:24. It seems that the witness is not the same person as the author of the Gospel, but that the author has received some of his first-hand information from this witness, that is, the disciple Jesus loved.

7. THE BURIAL
(1 9 : 3 8 - 4 2)

The body of Jesus, king in a kingdom not of this world, remained lifted up on the cross. The removal must, because of the Sabbath, precede sunset. Joseph of Arimathea, earlier a secret disciple for fear of his associates, went to Pilate and requested permission to take the body down. Apparently he is among those described in 12:42-43. "Nevertheless many, even of the authorities, believed in him. But because of the Pharisees they did not confess it, for fear that they would be put out of the synagogue; for they loved human glory more than the glory that comes from God." Nicodemus who came to Jesus at night (3:2) knew of Joseph's request and accompanied him. It is ironic that these two, secret admirers of Jesus, now make their veneration public, whereas the intimate disciples have scattered and discretely only met secretly (20:19). In defense of the disciples, however, it may be said that they had neither the connections nor the resources to initiate a burial in the manner of Joseph of Arimathea and Nicodemus. It is interesting that Pilate gave Joseph permission to take the body, but then that was the prerogative of relatives or friends that the Romans did not wish to preempt.

Joseph provided the newly hewn tomb and Nicodemus the burial spices. Both of these actions established the affluence of the two. These men prepared the body with one hundred Roman pounds (about 75 pounds) of spices for proper burial. They laid the body in a newly hewn nearby tomb in the garden, which according to Matthew 27:59 belonged to Joseph of Arimathea. Jesus secured two significant Jewish leaders of importance and wealth as disciples. They gave his body proper attention, regardless of the outcome. O'Day wrote, "Not only are the requirements of a proper Jewish burial adhered to, but also the combination of spices and linen burial clothes is normally accorded only to people of wealth or prominence (cf. the elegance of the Johannine description with Mark 15:46). The pristine condition of the garden tomb also underscores the dignity of this burial (v. 41)."[58]

For John what is significant is the sum total of Jewish leaders who affirmed Jesus whether known or incognito (John 12:42). According to Schnackenburg more significant than the wealth exhibited in Jesus' burial is the way in which God is at work. ". . . it matters just as much to him that, because of the circumstances, God has arranged things in this way. Because of the Jews' day of Preparation it is necessary to hurry. Now, the two men who, otherwise, followed Jesus only in secret, step forward resolutely. In clear contrast to the Jews (19:31, 38) they represent the fellowship of Jesus which shows great honor to its Lord."[59] John seemed not to relegate to a lower status those who were fearful of openly professing Jesus if they eventually exhibited such boldness.

[58] O'Day, p. 836.
[59] Schnackenburg, 3:295.

Jesus stated clearly that his
mission would continue
after being lifted up on the cross.
He also would be lifted from the tomb.

$\mathcal{L}ifted\ from$
$the\ \mathcal{T}omb$

(JOHN 20:1-31)

Jesus stated clearly that his mission would continue after being lifted up on the cross. He also would be lifted from the tomb. "For this reason the Father loves me, because I lay down my life in order to take it up again" (John 10:17). "I am the resurrection and the life. Those who believe in me, even though they die, will live, and everyone who lives and believes in me will never die" (John 11:25-26).

The resurrection section in John's Gospel is from 20:1–21:23. No one witnessed the resurrection as it unfolded, but Mary Magdalene, Peter, and the disciple Jesus loved looked into the tomb and found it empty. Afterward Jesus appeared to Mary Magdalene, ten of the disciples on the first evening, eleven of the disciples including Thomas a week later, and seven of the disciples at the Sea of Galilee. The empty tomb and the appearances of Jesus are the ultimate sign that he came from God and is returning to him. "I am ascending to my Father and your Father, and to my God and your God" (20:17).

It is perhaps because of the unparalleled victory of the resurrection that John does not set forth details of the deep distress the disciples experienced when Jesus died on the cross. Neither does he report the disappointment of the two disciples on the way to Emmaus found only in Luke. "But we had hoped that he was the one to redeem Israel" (Luke 24:21). Beasley-Murray wrote,

> The dreadful reality of the crucifixion crushed the followers of Jesus beyond measure, and their faith also . . . Moreover, it is highly probable that Jesus' predictions regarding his resurrection after three days were understood to refer to the resurrection when the kingdom of God came in glory in a short time (note Martha's response to 'Your brother will rise,' 11:24). The disciples would not

have envisaged a personal resurrection of Jesus, apart from
the resurrection to the kingdom of God in the last day.[60]

Whatever the inner turmoil of the disciples, they were baffled
by the empty tomb.

THE DISCOVERY
OF THE EMPTY TOMB
(20:1-11)

Mary Magdalene was the first to visit the tomb of Jesus, arriv-
ing while it was still dark. John does not tell us her purpose in coming. She soon discovered that the stone covering the entry had
been removed. The rolling of the stone probably required more
than one strong person. According to Matthew it was a great stone
(Matt. 27:60). Furthermore, at the instigation of the chief priests,
Pilate ordered that the stone be made as secure as possible, lest
someone steal the body (27:62-64). So the chief priests and their
guard of soldiers sealed the stone (Matt. 27:66). Mary's fear was
that the body of Jesus had been moved elsewhere to an unknown
site and she wouldn't know where to pay proper homage to her
deceased teacher. Mary did not look into the tomb at this time. She
concluded that if the stone had been rolled away then the body of
Jesus had been moved elsewhere (John 20:2).

After Mary Magdalene left the tomb she encountered Peter
and the other disciple who were apparently spending the night
somewhere near at hand. She told them about the open tomb and
her fear that the body was gone. She was greatly agitated, "They
have taken the Lord out of the tomb, and we do not know where
they have laid him" (20:2). She apparently either feared that the
owner of the tomb (in Matthew, Joseph of Arimathea) had
removed the body to another place, or perhaps even that grave
robbers had taken the body. That she used the word "we" shows
an awareness by John that other women were with her, though
John focuses on Mary alone (see also Matt. 28:1; Luke 24:10, where
other women are mentioned).

Peter and the other disciple hurried to the tomb to assess the

---

[60] Beasley-Murray, p. 371.

situation. The other disciple outran Peter and reached the tomb first. We are not told why, but perhaps the disciple Jesus loved was the younger of the two. We receive various hints in John, not found in the Synoptics, that the beloved disciple has priority over Peter. Notice 13:23 in which the disciple Jesus loved occupied the favored position at the meal. The age-old tradition is that the disciple Jesus loved was John, but this may be questioned if the beloved disciple lived in Jerusalem. When the beloved disciple looked in the tomb he did not go in, but saw the linen wrapping where the body should have been. He clearly waited for Peter showing him the deference. Peter, as he often did, did not hesitate, but pressed forward and entered the tomb. He saw the wrappings, and also the head covering which was rolled up in a place by itself (20:7).

The other disciple then entered pondering the implication of the body wrappings. When he grasped the situation, he believed. Why did the burial dressings lead him to believe? Beasley-Murray observed, "Chrysostom saw their pertinence [the wrappings] to the notion of robbery of the tomb: 'If anyone had removed the body, he would not have stripped it first, nor would he have taken the trouble to remove and roll up the napkin and put it in a place by itself' (In *Jo. Hom.* 85.4). One may add, nor would he have left those costly cloths and spices!"[61] John's concern may have been to draw out Christological implications. "Jesus has forsaken his burial clothes for ever, for he is risen! The Evangelist had penned the story of Lazarus, and recorded how Lazarus, at the bidding of Jesus, came forth from his tomb, with the wrappings of the dead still binding him hand and foot, and the napkin on his head; he had to be freed to take up life again in the world. Jesus on the contrary left his wrappings in the grave as a sign of his resurrection into the life of God's eternal order."[62] Peter, however, took some time to comprehend the ramifications of the scene before him.

The disciples were slow to recall that Jesus had quoted Scripture in which he foretold that he would rise from the dead, ". . . for as yet they did not understand the scripture that he must rise from the dead" (20:9).

---

[61] Ibid., p. 372.
[62] Ibid.

The Jews then said to him, "What sign can you show us for doing this?" Jesus answered them, "Destroy this temple, and in three days I will raise it up." The Jews then said, "This temple has been under construction for forty-six years, and will you raise it up in three days?" But he was speaking of the temple of his body. After he was raised from the dead, his disciples remembered that he had said this; and they believed the scripture and the word that Jesus had spoken (John 2:18-22).

Here was the sign that outdistanced all signs. As the result, the beloved disciple believed that Jesus was in fact, sent from God (2:8). He was the model disciple whose example challenged all to believe. His exemplary faith even out shown that of Peter.

THE APPEARANCE TO MARY MAGDALENE
(20:12-18)

Mary Magdalene returned with Peter and the other disciple, but stayed after they left and did not enter the tomb. She stood weeping outside. Perhaps now in hope against hope she pondered whether he indeed was "the resurrection and the life" (11:25). With the two gone she determined to look into the tomb. What did she hope to see? Perhaps she hoped that someone had returned the body. But she saw two angels.

Unlike Luke with many appearances of angels at the birth of Christ, and again at the tomb (Luke 24:4) these are the only angels that John reported anyone seeing. Jesus as Son of God takes the focus in this first appearance in John's Gospel. Mary sees an angel sitting at the head and another at the feet of where Jesus lay (20:12). "The presence of angels is a witness that the powers of heaven have been at work here. Their position in the tomb, one at the head and the other at the feet where Jesus had lain, is a reminder of the silent testimony of the grave clothes, but of another order; it witnesses that God, not robbers, has taken Jesus, for a purpose yet to be revealed."[63]

---

[63] Ibid., p. 374.

Neither Peter nor the other disciple saw the angels. The angels also appear only to the women in Luke (22:4), Mark (16:5), and Matthew (28:2). In Mark and Matthew an angel gives the women a message for the disciples that Jesus will meet them in Galilee. In Luke the angel reminds the women that Jesus spoke of his resurrection. In John the angels provide a prelude for the entrance of Jesus into Mary's presence. Jesus does not trespass upon humanity unannounced. John the Baptist heralded his arrival (John 1:6-9, 15), as now do the angels. The angels ask Mary why she is weeping. She replies that it is because they have taken away her Lord and she doesn't know where they have laid him. If only she could find the body she could pay proper respect and continue to weep appropriately.

As Mary spoke to the angels she sensed the presence of another. She turned around and behind her away from the tomb stood a man. The thought came to her that he was the gardener and he would know where the body of Jesus lay. Jesus asks Mary why she is weeping, the same question asked by the angels. She says to Jesus whom she supposed to be the gardener, "Sir, if you have carried him away, tell me where you have laid him, and I will take him away" (20:15). Mary probably doesn't have a place in mind where she will take him, but she likely intended to put the matter before the disciples. She herself, however, may have been a person of some means, and had access to family tombs. That she didn't know to whom she was speaking reminds one of the two disciples on the road to Emmaus whose "eyes were kept from recognizing Jesus" (Luke 24:16). Can Mary's eyes of identification also be darkened in regard to the resurrected Christ? The two, as Mary, were still darkened in mind in regard to Jesus' declaration that he would rise again on the third day. They did not have his prediction of resurrection at the forefront of their thinking. They only remembered his affirmation in that regard after they were convinced that he rose from the dead (John 2:22). We are also reminded of the fishermen in the boat who did not know who it was who addressed them from the shore until they pulled up a large catch of fish in their nets. All at once it dawned upon the disciple whom Jesus loved who it was who shouted, "Cast your net to the right side of the boat" (John 21:4-7).

After Mary poured out her concern for finding the body, Jesus spoke to her by name, "Mary." When he called out her name she was astonished (20:16). "Rabbouni!" she cried! One is reminded of Jesus' earlier declaration, "He calls his sheep by name" (10:3). She now responds to Jesus because she knows her teacher (shepherd). "The sheep follow him because they know his voice" (10:4).

Now that Mary acknowledges Jesus, he charges her with conveying a message to the disciples that will reveal where he is in the process of completing his mission. He first instructs her not to hold on to him since she probably had fallen at his feet. He must complete his mission unencumbered. "But go to my brothers and say to them, 'I am ascending to my Father and your Father, to my God and your God'" (20:17). Jesus was lifted up on the cross. He was lifted up from the tomb. Now he is to be lifted up to the Father. He promised the disciples that in his return to the Father he would prepare a place for them.

> If Mary is supposed to bring this message, word for word, to the disciples, it is easy to suppose that the disciples are meant to be reminded of other sayings of Jesus. If we look back in the gospel, the other passage that particularly comes to mind in this respect is 14:1-3, the beginning of the farewell discourse. Here alone is found the striking, "Believe in God!", and then follows the saying about the rooms in the Father's house. Jesus is going there to prepare a place for the disciple—a saying which lays the basis for the interpretation of Jesus' departure.[64]

Jesus is "ascending" to the Father through completing what he has promised. He is mediating with the Father full fellowship of the disciples with the Father. He is arranging for the sending of the *Paraklētos*—the Holy Spirit. He is continuing his prayer on their behalf so that they may engage in greater works and be filled with the ever-encircling love of God.

In his lifting up on the cross, in his lifting up from the tomb, in his lifting up to the Father, Jesus will draw all men to himself. Mary

---

[64] Schnackenburg, 3:318.

now set out for a meeting with the disciples and reported her discussion with Jesus. Mary Magdalene was the first to see the stone rolled away from the tomb. She was the first to see the risen Lord outside the tomb. She was no longer to look upon Jesus as God in the flesh, but as one arisen so that he could return to the Father. She was not to hold onto the pre-ascended Christ, but to bask in a new relationship with her ascended Lord!

THE APPEARANCE TO THE DISCIPLES THE FIRST NIGHT (20:19-23)

It is now the first day of the week. It has been an eventful day. Mary Magdalene went in the dark to weep before the sealed tomb of Jesus. But she was shocked to discover that the stone at the entrance of the tomb had been rolled away. She knew that though the disciples were distraught and without direction they still lingered in Jerusalem. She found Peter and the disciple Jesus loved and together they ran to the tomb. When they looked in they discovered the body missing and the wrapping materials essentially undisturbed. Not knowing what to make of this turn of events they left. Mary stayed around and when she looked into the tomb saw two angels. Still pondering what to make of this she turned and saw a man she took to be a gardener. She hoped he could tell her what had become of the body of Jesus. Rather, he addressed her as Mary and she knew it was the Lord. She went then to tell the gathered disciples, but they found her report incredulous. According to Luke, "But these words seemed to them an idle tale, and they did not believe them" (Luke 24:11).

That night the disciples gathered, perhaps trying to make sense of the bizarre events of the day. They perhaps too pondered what they should do, whether to stay in Jerusalem for a time or return to Galilee. The disciples met behind locked doors for they were fearful of the Jews. What were they to do? Where was the body of Jesus? Was there anything credible about Mary Magdalene's report that Jesus had talked with her? How could they get in touch with the Lord only Mary had seen? They didn't know where he had gone (14:5).

The disciples didn't need to find Jesus; he found them. Jesus

85

knew where they had gone. It was then the case and continues even until now that Jesus knows the location of those who are his. "Nathanael asked him, 'Where did you get to know me?' Jesus answered, 'I saw you under the fig tree before Philip called you'" (John 1:48). John's interest seems to be focused upon the need of the disciples to meet behind closed doors for fear of the Jews. At the same time the reader's attention is drawn to the fact that the resurrected Jesus entered into a secured room without disturbing its materiality. Jesus stood in the midst of the gathered group and said, "Peace be with you" (20:19). Locked doors could not keep him away. Despite now being biologically different, if not non-biological, the raised Christ exhibited continuity with the crucified Jesus. He showed the disciples his hands and his side. According to Luke, the disciples ". . . were startled and terrified, and they thought that they were seeing a ghost" (24:37). John does not say as much, but it was only after they saw Jesus' hands and side that "The disciples rejoiced when they saw the Lord" (John 20:20). Their fondest dream has been realized. Their Lord and master is alive!

Jesus repeated the greeting, "Peace be with you" (20:21). He employed the standard Jewish greeting Shalom. Not only his bodily appearance, but also his vocabulary is that of the earthly Jesus. In his departing discourses Jesus promised the disciples peace. "Peace I leave with you; my peace I give to you. I do not give to you as the world gives. Do not let your hearts be troubled, and do not let them be afraid" (John 14:27). Shalom in Hebrew means wellness, wholeness, a feeling of acceptance.

Jesus has fulfilled his mission on earth distant from the Father. Now he is on the verge of returning. His mission, however, is to be continued in those who are his. As God sent Jesus into the world, he likewise sends his disciples into the world. "So I send you" (20:21). Jesus discussed with his disciples the continuation of the ministry at his departure on prior occasions. "Very truly, I tell you, the one who believes in me will also do the works that I do and, in fact, will do greater works than these, because I am going to the Father" (John 14:12). "And now I am no longer in the world, but they are in the world, and I am coming to you. Holy Father, protect them in your name that you have given me, so that they may be one, as we are one" (John 17:11). With his "I send you", Jesus conferred upon the disciples a share in his own continuing ministry.

Jesus promised the disciples that they would be sent out empowered by the advocate or helper—the Holy Spirit. "And I will ask the Father, and he will give you another Advocate to be with you forever" (14:16). "But the Advocate, the Holy Spirit, whom the Father will send in my name, will teach you everything, and remind you of all that I have said to you" (14:26). "Nevertheless I tell you the truth: it is to your advantage that I go away, for if I do not go away, the Advocate will not come to you; but if I go I will send him to you" (John 16:7).

The disciples ministered along with Jesus when he was with them, but not under the auspices of the Holy Spirit. "Now he said this about the Spirit, which believers in him were to receive; for as yet there was no Spirit, because Jesus was not yet glorified" (John 7:39). Jesus was glorified in being lifted up. The time has now arrived for the bestowal of the Holy Spirit. After saying, "As the Father has sent me, so I send you," (20:21) Jesus breathed on the disciples and conferred the Holy Spirit. "Receive the Holy Spirit" (20:22).

The commentators have long struggled with how this bestowal of the Spirit in John 20:22 is to be understood in the light of the fall of the Holy Spirit upon the disciples at the feast of Pentecost as reported in Acts 2:1-21. In John Jesus' bestowal of the Spirit is in a private room with only the disciples present. It is comparable to the essentially private conferral of the Spirit upon Jesus at the commencement of his ministry (John 1:32-34). Luke emphasized the public bestowal of the Spirit at the opening up of the ministries in Jerusalem, all Judea and Samaria, and to the ends of the earth (Acts 1:8). The disciples received a public display of the fall of the Spirit in Jerusalem (Acts 2:21), in Judea and Samaria (Acts 8:15-17), and to the ends of the world, that is, to the Gentiles (Acts 10:44-48).

Not only were the disciples empowered for their ministry at the arrival of the Spirit, but likewise those who believed because of them (17:20). The longevity of Jesus' ministry extends beyond the first generation of disciples. This point is made again in John 20:29. In referring to Thomas, Jesus said, "Have you believed because you have seen me? Blessed are those who have not seen and yet have come to believe." Incidentally, the term, the twelve is not as important in the Gospel of John as in the Synoptics, occurring only three times as compared with ten in Mark. Various groups and commentators through the centuries have argued that the bestowal of the Spirit is either only for the earliest circles of Jesus' disciples or for those who occupy authorial positions in the churches down through the ages. I think the matter needs to be decided in the light of 1 John. First John focused upon the gifts of God to all Christians, not just to the first disciples. In writing to all the believers John declared, "But you have been anointed by the Holy One, and all of you have knowledge" (1 John 2:20). And again, "As for you, the anointing that you received from him abides in you, and so you do not need anyone to teach you. But your anointing teaches you about all things, and is true and is not a lie" (1 John 2:27). Notice how the affirmation in 1 John reads much like the statement of Jesus to the first disciples, "But the Advocate, the Holy Spirit, whom the Father will send in my name, will teach you everything, and remind you of all that I have said to you" (John 14:26). Before accepting human claims as to God-inspired proclamations, however, statements must be scrutinized in the light of the apostolic word. "Beloved, do not believe every spirit, but test the spirits to see whether they are of God . . . We are from God. Whoever knows God listens to us, and whoever is not from God does not listen to us. From this we know the spirit of truth and the spirit of error" (1 John 4:1-6).

Jesus also conferred upon the disciples the power to forgive sins. "If you forgive the sins of any, they are forgiven them; if you retain the sins of any, they are retained" (John 20:23). Jesus himself claimed the prerogative of forgiving sins. "I told you that you would die in your sins, for you will die in your sins unless you believe that I am he" (John 8:24). So the question is on whom did Jesus confer the privilege of forgiving sins? Is it only on those present in the locked room? Does the power extend to future authorial figures in the church? Can it also extend to any members of the body of believers? Is forgiveness of sins what results from being a part of the koinonia in the church? I believe that once again the answer may be forthcoming through what is expressed in 1 John. "But if we walk in the light as he himself is in the light, we have fellowship with one another, and the blood of Jesus his Son cleanses us from all sin" (1 John 1:7). The view of the church presupposed here is a high one indeed. Those who are in the fellowship, that is, the church of Jesus Christ, are forgiven of their sins by the blood of Jesus Christ. Those who have departed from the fellowship no longer have their sins forgiven. Departure from the fellowship may indeed be the sin unto death (1 John 5:16) since the sins of those departed are no longer being forgiven. This letter seems to have been written because of those who departed. "They went out from us, but they did not belong to us. . . ." (1 John 2:19).

The sense therefore that the church "dispenses" forgiveness of sins is a correct perception. But despite centuries of assertion that the church dispenses this forgiveness through special clergy, the perspective in 1 John is that Jesus parcels out forgiveness directly to those who have fellowship with God and Christ, the early disciples and with one another (1 John 1:1–2:2). The church of Jesus Christ in its fellowship is the place at which the blood of Christ may be apprehended and sins forgiven. O'Day's observations are right on.

First, Jesus' words in v. 23 are addressed to the entire faith community, not to its apostolic leaders. Any discussion of this verse, therefore, must be grounded in an understanding of forgiveness of sins as the work of the entire community. Second, the community's enactment of Jesus' words in v. 23 depends on both Jesus' words of sending in v. 21 and the gift of the Holy Spirit in v. 22. The forgiveness of sins must be understood as the Spirit-empowered mission of continuing Jesus' work in the world.[65]

THE APPEARANCE A WEEK LATER WITH THOMAS PRESENT (20:24-29)

Thomas is mentioned in John more than in the other Gospels. In the naming of those going fishing with Peter, Thomas is mentioned first (John 21:2). Down through history he has received the appellation "doubting Thomas" perhaps not altogether fairly. The first time we read about Thomas in John is when Jesus has decid-

---

[65] O'Day, p. 847.

ed to take another trip to Jerusalem. Some of the disciples were visibly shaken when Jesus made this announcement. "Rabbi, the Jews were just now trying to stone you, and are you going there again?" (John 11:8). The bold one, willing to go wherever Jesus desired was Thomas. "Thomas, who was called the Twin, said to his fellow disciples, 'Let us also go, that we may die with him'" (John 11:16). In the next situation Thomas among the disciples is forthright in declaring his failure to comprehend. After Jesus stated that the disciples knew "the way to the place I am going" Thomas burst out, "Lord, we do not know where you are going. How can we know the way?" (John 14:5). Thomas exhibited a certain close-to-the-facts, empirical mentality.

In our churches today we have disciples both of the disposition of Peter and of Thomas. Some of us, more in the mold of Thomas, dread the impetuous and demanding commitments of a Peter. Perhaps what these people of this sort propose, a friendship day or a weekend seminar, is a worthy undertaking. But we dread to see it coming. We know that often the person who commits the rest of us either is unwilling or unable to orchestrate and implement the proposed activities. It takes someone like Thomas who asks the hard questions and who is willing to enlist others, plan and put in the hours who brings a friendship day to reality. But the church needs people after the style of Peter otherwise the people of God will be stuck on dead center. And the church needs the realistic hard-working Thomases otherwise the proposed body-building activities will flounder.

Thomas was not with the disciples the first time Jesus appeared. We do not know the reason for his absence. But we presume it was not because he was fearful. He was, as we noted, the one prepared to go to Jerusalem and die if it came to that (11:16). Thomas was not always as perceptive of who Jesus was and what he taught as his Lord may have wished, but he was not alone in that regard (14:5). He was hesitant to accept the other disciples' claim that the risen Lord had been in their midst. A living Jesus was so incredible that he had to see for himself. "Unless I see the mark of the nails in his hands, and put my finger in the mark of the nails and my hand in his side, I will not believe" (20:25). What he requested, however, was exactly what Jesus offered to his disciples in the first visit (20:20).

Even doubting Thomas with his high demands discovered his doubt evaporating when standing face to face with Jesus. Jesus requested that Thomas put his finger on his hands and his hand on his side. As far as the text informs us Thomas did not pursue that request. The presence of Jesus was so indisputable and numinous that all Thomas could do was simply utter the confession, "My Lord and my God!" (20:28). We may infer at this point that Thomas has comprehended what before was opaque to him. "If you know me, you will know my Father also. From now on you do know him and have seen him" (John 14:7). "After the overpowering impression made on Thomas by Jesus' appearance with the doors closed, the knowledge concerning his demand, and the words of Jesus directed to him personally, the disciple can only just utter this confession which testifies to personal emotion."[66]

Jesus' reaction was not fully what we might expect. In a sense he commended Thomas, but he went on to express a greater admiration for those who depended upon the word of witness given by the original disciples. "Jesus said to him, 'Have you believed because you have seen me? Blessed are those who have not seen and yet have come to believe'" (John 20:29). Sight may not lead to faith, but to the pursuit of physical fulfillment (John 6:2). Sight brought Thomas to faith and such is commendable. But faith built upon the testimony of those who saw—faith established upon the Word is especially commendable. John is written to build faith among those who are distant from the first believers in both time and space. "But these are written so that you may come to believe that Jesus is the Messiah, the Son of God, and that through believing you may have life in his name" (John 20:31).

Jesus expressed his admiration, not only of those who like Thomas actually saw him, but also those who will later come to believe. Their faith was not based on their own experience face to face with the Lord, but upon the witness of those who heard the stories told by the first witnesses.

O'Day aptly wrote,

---

[66] Schnackenburg, 3:332.

The Johannine Easter narratives are a reminder that the church's life is ultimately bound to Jesus' life, death, and resurrection. To celebrate the resurrection, the Fourth Gospel suggests, is also to celebrate the beginning of the church's mission in the world. Jesus lives, not because he can walk through locked doors and show his wounds to frightened disciples, but because he breathes new life into those disciples through the gift of the Spirit and commissions them to continue his work.[67]

A CONCLUDING REMARK
(20:30-31)

Clearly John 20:30-31 is a summary and conclusion. The question is to what is it a conclusion? In the first eighteen centuries of the Gospel's existence the assumption was that these verses conclude the stories alone in John 20. Chapter 21 was taken to be the conclusion to the whole Gospel. That has not, however, been the consensus view more recently. The common current view is that 20:30-31 is a conclusion to the Gospel and chapter 21 is an addendum. O'Day presents detailed claims for 20:30-31 being the conclusion to the signs in chapter 20.[68] I think she is correct about the resurrection appearances being signs, as I have argued throughout this book. I am still inclined, however, to think that the signs under consideration are those distributed throughout chapters 1 through 20 because of the interest in signs from the first, and that "the signs written in this book" encompass more than the signs in chapter 20.[69]

John declares that he wrote so as to set out some of the many signs that Jesus did in order that those who heard and read might come to "believe that Jesus is the Messiah, the Son of God" (20:31). Scholars differ over whether this conclusion implies that John's targeted audience is those who have not yet come to believe or those believers whose faith needs deepening. The expression in the Greek perhaps lends more support to the latter, but may be read either way. Beasley-Murray concluded, "It is increasingly recog-

---

[67] O'Day, p. 848.
[68] Ibid., pp. 850-852.
[69] Keener is of the same opinion, p. 1213.

nized, however, that a decision like this can hardly rest on a fine point of Greek grammar, not least in view of the fact that the Evangelist does not always keep the rules in his use of tenses."[70] Furthermore, the focus in the Gospel upon the trauma of being cast out of the synagogue gives the weight to those who already believe. Keener concluded, "Throughout the Gospel, many people become initial believers, but their initial faith proves insufficient with perseverance (2:23-25; 8:30, 59). John's goal is not simply initial faith but persevering faith, and discipleship (8:30-32; 15:4-7). John's purpose is to address believers at a lesser stage of discipleship and to invite them to persevere as true disciples."[71] Nevertheless, the end result is that those convinced of Jesus' Messiahship are sent to share that faith with the world for whom Jesus, the Son of God, died.

John is convinced that the signs elicit a decisive commitment in favor of a heavenly provenance and mission of Jesus. The signs more immediate to this declaration are the empty tomb, the appearance to Mary Magdalene and Jesus calling her by name, the appearance to the disciples in a locked room a week later, and after that to the disciples with Thomas present. Thomas' confession is particularly noteworthy, "My Lord and my God." In 20:30 the signs lead to the belief that Jesus is the Messiah, that is, the anointed one, the king of a transcendental kingship (John 18:36). Furthermore, he is the Son of God. The end result of such belief is "through believing you may have life through his name (21:31). "For God so loved the world that he gave his only Son, so that everyone who believes in him may not perish but may have eternal life" (3:16).

---

[70] Beasley-Murray, p. 387.
[71] Keener, p. 1216.

*The point is that when Jesus feeds,
the supply is more than sufficient.*

$\mathcal{C}$oncluding $\mathcal{M}$atters: $\mathcal{T}$he $\mathcal{A}$ppearance in $\mathcal{G}$alilee

(JOHN 21)

Chapter 21 in the past several decades has been identified as a later addition or an appendix to the Gospel even if by John the son of Zebedee. But such a conclusion is not necessary in view of the characteristics of ancient documents as Keener has shown.[72] Furthermore, the style and especially several trajectories in 1–20 continue throughout Chapter 21, and some of the details in this last chapter, especially references to the disciple Jesus loved, provide additional insight to the whole Gospel.

Jesus has been glorified. The ultimate signs to establish Jesus' identity are his being lifted up on the cross and from the tomb, as well as his appearances after he arose (2:18-22). The signs pointing to Jesus as raised from the dead in chapter 20 all occurred in the environs of Jerusalem. Chapter 21 continues the appearances of the risen Christ "After these things Jesus showed himself again to the disciples . . .", this time in Galilee by the sea of Tiberias. Both Matthew (28:16) and Mark (16:7) report that Jesus appeared to his disciples in Galilee after he requested that they meet there. The Synoptics only report one visit of Jesus to Jerusalem after he commences his ministry, that is, the one in which he is crucified. Luke, of course, relates an encounter of Jesus with the teachers at the temple when he was twelve (Luke 2:41-46). John in contrast reports at least four trips of Jesus to Jerusalem prior to his last.

One reason for thinking that John is historically correct in this regard is that it seems quite surprising that suddenly the twelve disciples of Jesus, all Galileans, transferred their base of operation

---

[72] Keener, p. 1221f; see also O'Day who argues for the chapter 21 as a part of the Gospel, pp. 854-855.

from Galilee to Jerusalem apart from prior acquaintance with the city. Furthermore in the Gospel of John several disciples of Jesus are residents of the city and vicinity, specifically Lazarus, Mary, Martha (John 11), Joseph of Arimathea, Nicodemus (John 19:38-42), perhaps the disciple Jesus loved and many others unnamed (John 12:42-43). The multiple visits and prior acquaintances that John reports make such a transfer by the time of first Pentecost after the resurrection much more plausible. According to Luke, Jesus declared that the disciples were to begin their ministry, not from Galilee, but Jerusalem. ". . . repentance and forgiveness of sins is to be proclaimed in his name to all nations, beginning from Jerusalem" (Luke 24:47). The declaration of Jesus we may presume was the main impetus behind the move.

FISHING IN GALILEE
(21:1-14)

Simon Peter, Thomas, Nathanael, the sons of Zebedee, that is, James and John, with two others, were in Galilee and upon Peter's instigation, decide to go fishing. The number totaled seven, which may represent the coming church, as in Revelation 2-3 where seven churches are named. One of the unnamed may be the disciple Jesus loved because he was on the boat (21:7).

Not as much is made of the disciples fishing in John as in the Synoptics. In fact, it is only in chapter 21 that the disciples are said to go fishing. Fish, however, for human consumption are mentioned earlier in John. In the account of Jesus feeding the multitudes, loaves and fishes comprise the food. Jesus fed the five thousand fish and bread starting with only two fish, and five loaves of bread. When the meal was over they gathered up twelve baskets of remains (John 6:9-14). Whenever anyone eats with Jesus, no one goes away hungry or thirsty for that matter (2:6-10). That Jesus himself provides adequate nourishment is already affirmed in chapter 6:52-58. Jesus declared that those God has given him are nurtured by eating his body and blood—that is, the bread and the fruit of the vine (John 6:57-58).

Despite having fished all night, the disciples caught nothing. We are reminded of the Lukan account of the time at which Jesus called Peter, James and John. In that instance likewise the three had fished all night and caught nothing. Jesus told Peter to go out into the deep water and let the nets down. When he complied with the injunction of Jesus he caught so many fish that he called out for James and John to row out and load some of the fish on their boat. When the fishermen completed the task both boats were filled (Luke 5:4-7). Does this convey the message that only when Jesus directs the believers do they catch an abundance of fish?

After daybreak Jesus stood on the beach, but the disciples didn't recognize him even though he had already appeared to them after his resurrection. He was distant and neither they did recognize his voice. They were much like the two disciples on the road to Emmaus whose "eyes were kept from recognizing him." Jesus inquired of them "Children, you have no fish, have you?" Jesus even addressed the disciples in the same manner as at the dinner after which he washed their feet. "Little children, I am with you only a little longer" (13:33). The vocabulary of the risen Christ is the same as that of Jesus with whom they journeyed to Jerusalem. But still they did not recognize their Teacher and Lord (13:13).

Crestfallen by the absence of a catch, the disciples can only concur. No, they had not caught any fish! Jesus now instructed them to cast their net to the right side of the boat. Even then, though a disciple is to know the master's voice (John 10:4), their ears were blocked.

This time when they cast their net and drew it toward them, it was so loaded with fish that they could not haul it in (21:6). When Jesus gives an order unexpected results accrue. It now dawned on the disciple Jesus loved that the command could only have come from Jesus, so he exclaimed to Peter, "It is the Lord!" (21:7). The disciple Jesus loved was the consummate disciple since "his sheep know his voice" (10:4). Peter hurriedly put on his clothes, jumped into the sea and headed for shore. The rest of the disciples brought in the boat dragging behind it the huge load of fish. They were only about a hundred yards from shore.

Once the disciples landed they discovered that Jesus had a charcoal fire glowing with fish cooking over it as well as bread. The previous time at which Peter stood near a charcoal fire he was in the courtyard of the high priest. It was at that prior fire that he denied three times having been with his Lord. Peter, because he has been in the presence of his Lord at least twice after the resurrection, has regained his old confidence, if not impetuosity. Jesus instructed the disciples to bring some of the fish they had just caught to add to what he already was cooking (21:9). The disciples still have need for food, and just as Jesus fed the multitudes he now feeds the disciples—once again bread and fish. Peter did not hesitate. He went aboard the boat and hauled the net with its catch ashore. "There is an underlying irony to this [request for food], because Jesus initiates his contact with the disciples by asking them for food, but in the end will give food to them (vv. 9, 12-13). This pattern recalls Jesus' exchange with the Samaritan woman in John 4:7-16. Jesus initially requested a drink from the woman (4:7), but in the end he offered her living water (4:13-14)."[73]

The net was remarkably full with a hundred and fifty three large fish. Much intellect has been exerted and ink exhausted through the centuries to discern the significance of 153. But all this ingenuity may miss the point. The fact however that a concrete number is cited seems to invite symbolism. The question arises as to what that symbolism might be. Unquestionably Jesus performed a great miracle. Jerome (AD 345–420) proposed a somewhat literalistic symbolism. He argued that Greek and Roman biologists classified 153 kinds of fish. This enormous catch therefore incorporated all species of fish and thereupon the totality of the church. Similarly the catch of people by the disciples is to include all of humankind. Unfortunately, Jerome's sources cannot be checked out and the extant listings do not identify 153 kinds.[74]

Augustine (AD 354–430) proposed two ways of understanding the number. He first observed that the numbers 1 through 17 added totals 153 and since this is a triangular number suggests completeness. Also 17 is ten, that is the number of the ten commandments, plus seven which stands for the sevenfold Spirit of God (Rev. 1:4). In his second proposal Augustine suggested an allegorical meaning. This number he declared is a symbol for the Trinity (153 = 3 X 50 + 3). Cyril of Alexander (who died AD 444) held that 100 represented the fullness of the Gentiles, 50 the rem-

---

[73] O'Day, p. 857.
[74] Keener, p. 1232.

nant of the Jews (Rom. 11:25-26), and 3 the number of the Trinity.

Another approach both ancient and modern is that the number stands for some name or set of words. This approach is designated gematria. Beasley-Murray wrote, "Gematria is a term derived from geometry, but it makes a play with words in languages wherein numerals are represented by letters of the alphabet (a = 1, b = 2, c = 3, etc.). Both the Greeks and Hebrews represented numbers in this way; accordingly any name (or even any word) could be added up and represent by it total."[75] One such number is 666 the designation of the anti-Christ in Revelation 13:18. Many commentators conclude that this is the numerical equivalent of "Nero Caesar" written in the Hebrew alphabet. Some suggest that the numerical value of 153 is "children of God", that is, those who the disciples will convey into the heavenly kingdom. Another proposal is that the number is equivalent to Nathanael gamma, that is the third appearance of Jesus to Nathanael, or that it is the number for "alpha Maria" the first Mary the mother of the Lord who provides sustenance to the united church. Another suggestion is that the number is equivalent to Mount Pisgah and just as in his departure Moses passed on his leadership to Joshua and Israel, so Jesus passed on his leadership to Peter.[76]

All of these suggestions, however, may miss the actual reason for mentioning 153. The reason may be much simpler. The specific identification of 153 fish may simply mean that an eyewitness was so impressed that he counted the fish. The number and size of the fish in itself is impressive and pregnant with meaning.

The point is that when Jesus feeds, the supply is more than sufficient. When the 5,000 were fed every one ate to their fill and 12 baskets of remains were taken up. Jesus started with two fish; the catch of the disciples was 153. Jesus proclaimed that the disciples would do greater works (14:12). The disciples are to feed the flock of God with the bounty that he supplies. Jesus trained twelve; the disciples will train many more. These disciples and their converts can feed others because their Lord has provided beforehand with

---

[75] Beasley-Murray, p. 402.
[76] Keener, p. 1231; Beasley-Murray, pp. 410-414.

great abundance. From the first John announced the copiousness of the gifts of Jesus. "From his fullness we have all received, grace upon grace" (John 1:16). "I am the bread of life. Whoever comes to me will never be hungry, and whoever believes in me will never be thirsty" (6:35). "I am the gate. Whoever enters by me will be saved, and will come in and go out and find pasture" (John 10:9).

The disciples, and apparently Jesus, ate the fish. Can Jesus digest fish in his resurrection body? According to Paul "flesh and blood cannot inherit the kingdom of God" (1 Cor. 15:50). But what is impossible for humans may be possible for deity. According to Genesis 18:1 "The Lord appeared to Abraham by the oaks of Mamre." More specifically three men showed up at his tent (Gen. 18:2). Abraham hastened and prepared a meal for the three of bread, curds, milk and a calf (Gen. 18:6-8). He watched them while they ate. So the Hebrews writer declared, "Do not neglect to show hospitality of strangers, for by doing that some have entertained angels without knowing it" (Heb. 13:2).

Even though the disciples knew that it was Jesus in their midst they did not ask questions. The aura of the one who had died and now ate breakfast with them was too overpowering for serious theological discussion or small talk. This is the third time Jesus appeared to the disciples (21:14). Jesus affirmed three times that he was Jesus of Nazareth (18:4-7). Peter denied three times that he was a disciple of Jesus (18:17-26). Now Jesus appeared three times to the disciples after his resurrection (21:14). Three times is an adequate proof or sign that Jesus was sent from God and is returning to him. Soon the final stage of his lifting up will be accomplished.

THE CHARGE TO PETER
(21:15-19)

The Gospel now takes up the role of Peter and the disciple Jesus loved in the coming community of faith, that is, the church. Each will have crucial but complementary roles.

When the breakfast was over Jesus engaged Peter in conversation. He bluntly asked Peter, "Simon son of John, do you love (*agapaō*) me more than these?" (21:15). It is interesting that Jesus asks "more than these" since Peter declared earlier upon Jesus' announcement that he was leaving, "Lord, why can I not follow you now? I will lay down my life for you" (John 13:37). His boast then seems to imply that whatever the fate of the others he should be permitted to go with Jesus.[77] Now in response to the pointed question Peter answered, "Yes Lord, you know that I love (*phileō*) you" (21:15). Jesus responded, "Feed my Lambs." A second time Jesus asked him, "Do you love (*agapaō*) me?" Peter responded, "Yes, Lord; you know that I love (*phileō*) you" (21:16). Jesus charged him, "Tend my sheep." A third time Jesus asked, "Do you love (*phileō*) me?" Peter now perturbed, and hurt, exclaimed, "You know that I love (*phileō*) you." Jesus declared a third time, "Feed my sheep" (21:17). The text seems to imply that Peter was hurt by the third question because he denied his Lord three times and now he is forced by Jesus to declare his love for him three times. Perhaps the Lord's questions are designed to release Peter from the guilt of his denial, because after the third time Jesus ceased asking him the question. Jesus accepted Peter despite his having caved in during the hours of arrest, indictment and crucifixion.

Some students of Greek have noted that Jesus employed one Greek work *agapaō* for love and Peter another, *phileō*. Some scholars declare that *agapaō* is a more demanding form of love than *phileō* because it requires a giving up. *Phileō* on the other hand is like the love of brothers for each other and not as exacting. Peter was not yet ready, so it is said, for the ultimate decision of giving up self as Jesus requested. Furthermore, the third time, inasmuch as Peter responded *phileō* to the first two questions, Jesus finally accepted the lesser love—*phileō*—from Peter. Peter was hurt that Jesus lowered his expectation because of Peter's unwillingness to make the deeper commitment. This sounds good and preaches. But it may not be the case.

Certainly the three times Jesus questioned Peter are important. In fact the text declares that Peter was hurt, not because of the Greek word Jesus used, but because he asked him the third time (21:17). I think the change in verbs is a matter of style not of the quality of love. In a parallel case when Jesus charges Peter to feed the sheep three times, the Greek words are varied in each case.

---

[77] Beasley-Murray declared that Jesus is asking about the depth of his love, however, not to compare himself with the other disciples, p. 405.

O'Day examined the use of *agapaō* and *phileō* in the Gospel of John and concluded that these two Greek words are employed interchangeably. "These verbs are used as synonyms throughout the Gospel, with no difference in meaning. For example both verbs are used to speak of the disciple whom Jesus loved (*ēgapa*, 13:23; *ephilei*, 20:2); God's love for Jesus (*agapa*, 10:17; *philei*, 5:20). . . . There is no reason, therefore, to ascribe gradations of meaning to their usage here (as the NIV does)."[78]

We now turn to Jesus' charge to Peter. After asking Peter if he loved him Jesus responds with (1) "Feed my lambs", (2) "Tend my sheep", and (3) "Feed my sheep". The vocabulary here also has variety, but apparently again for stylistic not substantive purposes. The meaning in each case regardless of the vocabulary is essentially the same. What is significant is that the disciples who have been fed by Jesus are in turn to feed those who accept Jesus because of the apostolic witness. Just as Jesus fed the multitudes loaves and fishes, and the disciples caught adequate fish to supply the seven and many more, so Peter and the rest are instructed out of the copiousness of Jesus' provisions to feed his sheep. They are challenged to be fishers of men (Luke 5:10). Just as Peter hauled in the fish (21:11) so he and the disciples (21:8) are to join Jesus and God in drawing in the people. "And I, when I am lifted up from the earth, will draw all people to myself" (John 12:32). Like master, like servant. Just as the master gave his life for the sheep (10:11), so also will Peter (21:18, 19).

The question now comes to the forefront as it has through much of Christian history as to whether Peter here is assigned a unique function of the same order as that in Matthew 16. "And I tell you, you are Peter, and on this rock I will build my church, and the gates of Hades will not prevail against it. I will give you the keys of the kingdom of heaven, and whatever you bind on earth will be bound in heaven, and whatever you loose on earth will be loosed in heaven" (Matt. 16:18-20). The question may be raised even in regard to the Matthew comment as to whether it singularly identifies Peter for the role specified. At least it is clear from Acts 15 that when the question of circumcising confronted the church the gath-

---

[78] O'Day, p. 860; also Keener, pp. 1235-1236; Schnackenburg especially attributes the different vocabulary to style, 3:361.

ering consisted of apostles and elders. Peter was the first to speak on behalf of the acceptance of the uncircumcised (Acts 15:6-7), but he was neither in charge of the meeting nor did he issue a unilateral proclamation. James made the statement that brought the meeting to a conclusion (Acts 15:13) and declared his decision in regard to the matter. After James' statement the text declares, "Then the apostles and the elders with the consent of the whole church, decided to choose men from among their members and to send them to Antioch with Paul and Barnabus" (Acts 15:22).[79]

In the Gospel of John whenever Jesus charged the disciples with their future mission he never singularly separated Peter from the rest. "As you have sent me into the world, so I have sent them into the world. And for their sakes I sanctify myself, so that they also may be sanctified" (John 17:18). So Peter is charged to feed the lambs so as to be a model for all disciples. Peter is to feed the followers of Christ because Christ loved his disciples and instructed them to love one another. "I give you a new commandment, that you love one another. Just as I have loved you, you also should love one another. By this everyone will know that you are my disciples, if you have love for one another" (John 13:34-35). This is a manifesto to all the disciples. Their assignment is to be concretely carried out through feeding the flock of the Lord. The disciples are to love the sheep as the Lord loved them. "I am the good shepherd. The good shepherd lays down his life for the sheep" (John 10:11).

We take up now Jesus' prediction concerning the death of Peter (21:18-19). Jesus' depiction of Peter's death involves the stretching out his hands, having a belt fastened around him, and being forced to go to a certain location against his own wishes. Mel Gibson's *The Passion of the Christ* should enable one to envision what was to happen to Peter. Jesus predicted that he would be crucified. The arms were bound with rope to the cross bar as well as nailed. A rope or belt may have encircled the body. Such a description is also given in regard to Jesus' death (John 18:2).

Peter's death is to be like that of the Lord's, "the kind of death by which he would glorify God" (John 21:19). "Now the Son of

---

[79] But see Raymond Brown in his John commentary (2:1114-1116) who argues that the church should be governed by one pastor.

Man has been glorified, and God has been glorified in him" (John 13:31). After making this somewhat cryptic affirmation to Peter, Jesus decreed, "Follow me." Whenever Jesus called disciples he asked them to follow. "He found Philip and said to him, 'Follow me'" (1:43). Jesus' sheep follow him, "My sheep hear my voice. I know them, and they follow me" (John 10:27). His servants follow. "Whoever serves me must follow me, and where I am, there will my servant be also. Whoever serves me, the Father will honor" (John 12:26). Earlier Jesus told Peter he could not follow him in the anguishing hours of his death. But he would follow later. "Simon Peter said to him, 'Lord, where are you going?' Jesus answered, 'Where I am going, you cannot follow me now; but you will follow afterward.'" (John 13:36). Jesus is now calling Peter to follow even all the way to his own cross. Previously Peter expressed his willingness to lay down his life (13:38), a boast that Jesus rejected. He will now be able to do what he could not do formerly, that is, lay down his life in love. O'Day concluded, "Peter like the beloved disciple, is to be known by his share in Jesus' love. Peter's authority for the readers of the Fourth Gospel thus does not derive from his 'office,' but from the fullness of his love for Jesus and Jesus' hour."[80]

PETER AND THE OTHER DISCIPLE (21:20-23)

After Jesus told Peter, "Follow me," Peter turned and saw the disciple Jesus loved following them. That disciple too was obviously a "follower." He is identified as the "the one who had reclined next to Jesus at the supper" (John 13:23). In that setting this disciple was closer to Jesus than was Peter. Since he is only identified in the Gospel of John as the disciple Jesus loved, it is obvious that he had special significance to the Johannine circle of churches. This circle was most probably situated in the Roman province of Asia comprised at minimum by the seven churches mentioned in Revelation 2–3.

Peter asked Jesus to comment on the beloved disciple wondering whether death on the cross would also be his fate. Peter may have fretted over whether this disciple might be shown

---

[80] O'Day, p. 862.

favoritism, and Jesus' reply may imply as much. "If it is my will that he remain until I come, what is that to you" (John 21:22). Disciples need to keep their eyes on Jesus not on their fellows. So Jesus again enjoined Peter, "Follow me!" What counted with Jesus was not how long one followed, but whether there was a willingness to follow, even unto death. Because of Jesus' remark, a rumor circulated that by making it Jesus hinted that the disciple he loved would live until he returned (21:23).

In v. 24, the narrator makes sure that the reader recognizes that even though the beloved disciple does not die a martyr's death, he nonetheless bears witness to Jesus. His witness is the foundation of the very Gospel through which the readers experience Jesus. The beloved disciple's death does not diminish his standing in the community, because his witness remains. Peter's ministry is marked by his death; the beloved disciple's is marked by this Gospel.[81]

THE AUTHENTICITY OF THE GOSPEL (21:24-25)

The Gospel ends with the attestation that what is here written is true. It is true because it includes the eyewitness account provided by the disciple Jesus loved. That is this disciple's importance to this Gospel. The declaration seems to assume that the Gospel of John author and the disciple Jesus loved are two different people. The implication seems to be that by the time this Gospel was completed both Peter and the disciple Jesus loved were deceased.

Jesus did many other things only some of which are reported in this book. If every last action of Jesus had been written down, the author opines that the world could not contain the books. He believed, however, that the mighty works and declarations (signs) he did set forth were adequate to establish the conclusion that Jesus is the Messiah, the Son of God. "But these are written so that you may come to believe that Jesus is the Messiah, the Son of God, and that through believing you may have life in his name" (John 20:30, 31).

[81] Ibid.

The Gospel of John is a great boon.
By reading it faith is intensified and
through believing in Jesus
a new quality of life is attained.

Why Ponder over the Gospel of John?

9

Why should we spend our invaluable time pondering the details in the Gospel of John? The author's own answer is, "Now Jesus did many other signs in the presence of his disciples, which are not written in this book. But these are written so that you may come to believe that Jesus is the Messiah the Son of God, and that through believing you may have life in his name" (John 20:30-31). The Gospel of John is a great boon. By reading it faith is intensified and through believing in Jesus a new quality of life is attained. "I came that they may have life, and have it abundantly" (John 10:10). The born-from-above life makes a salutary difference even now, but also forever. "I give them eternal life, and they will never perish" (John 10:28).

What about faith in Christ in our time? Are circumstances such that believing that Jesus Christ is the Son of God is difficult? In many ways the American scene is becoming increasingly secular. Especially in terms of lifestyle Americans are turning their backs on norms once considered Christian in regard to sexual relationships and preferences. Americans have become unrestrained in regard to chemical highs of all sorts. Increasingly, ethical guidelines, once considered Christian, no longer determine what happens in the business world. Because of these departures from standard Christian morals and ethics, is it becoming increasingly difficult to believe that Jesus created every entity that was created?

I myself find the answer somewhat surprising. Actually it may be more respectable now than in the days of my youth in many circles to believe in Christ. That's not to say that a higher percentage of people do. The numbers are going down. But especially among people under forty it is increasingly acceptable to believe whatever one wants to believe and be public about it without recrimination as long as one does not try to force one's beliefs on others.

When I was a young adult almost no one attributed artistic skills to God. These days in programs for Broadway plays, major musical productions and operas certain stars thank both God and sometimes their parents for encouraging and sustaining their talents. In sporting events various athletes point skyward as a word of thanks and attribution to God. Even politicians have concluded that declaring oneself a believer augments voter support.

Even so, a vibrant faith is not easily sustained. We are surrounded by too many distractions regarding work, family, recreation and entertainment. Despite our stated faith, we suffer periods of emptiness and ennui. We are sometimes depressed, stressed, and burned out. We seem to have few resources for deep, constant joy, conviction or the energy to move ahead. Sometimes we only faintly hear the call of Jesus "Follow me." The clarity of his voice has been muted by the distractions. I am reminded of the century and a half-old hymn, "Jesus Calls Us."

Jesus calls us: o'er the tumult Of our life's wild restless sea,
Day by day His sweet voice soundeth, Saying "Christian, follow me."

Jesus calls us from the worship of the vain world's golden store:
From each idol that would keep us, Saying, "Christian love me more."

In our joys and in our sorrows, Days of toil, and hours of ease,
Still He calls, in cares and pleasures, "Christian, love me more than these."

John is the book for us in times like these. We are reminded through what is immediate that the demands for water, food and relationships are real. Behind these realities is their creator and "without him not one thing came into being" (John 1:3). John presents us with the challenge of locating behind and beyond the ordinary, God at work and His Son at work. John, more than the other

Gospels, encourages us to see the signs of God's presence where most people only discern routine natural causes. That is why John's Gospel is for us—we who believe. We need to move up to the next level. John arranges for this ascent, not through emotional outbursts or tight-jawed, stomach-firmed-up affirmations. He invites us to observe the details of Jesus' life to ascertain whether there are telltale signs of deity. He invites his readers to an inductive reflection upon the uncommon works and words of Christ that point to a reality beyond. John has little time for a mindless faith that simply affirms regardless of reasons or facts. What he reports is not ephemeral. He erects and commends a lasting faith, not one that is here today and gone tomorrow.

The dimension of transcendence so often missing from American life is much in prominence in other parts of the world. Many persons in contemporary America may be inclined toward faith. But the achieving of a vibrant faith is often closed off because of a century-old skepticism regarding signs of the work of God in the encountered world. Persons in third-world countries in Africa, Asia, and South America do not face the same hurdles. They are much more inclined to envision God at work in many aspects of that which surrounds them. It is for that reason that disciples in these countries are rapidly expanding while in America mainstream groups are doing well to hold their own. Growth in Churches of Christ in the past two decades has largely been confined to third-world countries. In Africa there are now about 800,000 members. In India there may be more than 1,000,000. In South America the numbers may exceed 200,000. There are now more members of Churches of Christ outside of North America than on this continent.

The Gospel of John read carefully provides numerous faith-building episodes regarding Jesus' unprecedented comments and actions. I have argued that Jesus' comments as well as his actions are "signs" pointing to his heavenly provenance.

The extraordinary remarks of Jesus or those of others about him add up, leading to the conclusion that Jesus indeed, as he claimed was God's Son (John 10:36). One of Jesus' early disciples Nathanael, who when he first heard of Jesus asked, "Can anything good come out of Nazareth?" (John 1:46). Despite Nathanael's initial reservations he was impressed when Jesus told him, "I saw you under the fig tree before Philip called you" (John 1:48). Nicodemus recognized something extraordinary when Jesus told him, "No one can see the kingdom of God without being born from above" (John 3:3). He and many other contemporaries of Jesus came to experience the birth of which Jesus spoke (John 19:38-42). John the Baptist witnessed to the Holy Spirit falling upon Jesus like a dove and remaining (John 1:32). Later Jesus went across the Jordan where John the Baptist had been baptizing and many came to him there. They said, "Everything John said about this man was true" (John 10:41).

Jesus breathed the same Spirit upon the disciples (John 20:22) and their future accomplishments were inestimable, both as attested in Acts and three centuries later by Eusebius (AD 260–340). The woman at the well in Samaria was impressed when Jesus told her, "For you have had five husbands, and the one you have now is not your husband" (4:18). She reported to her fellow countrymen, "He told me everything I have ever done" (4:39). Jesus was able to avoid some detractors and willingly tolerate the presence of others involved in God's plan because he "knew from the first who were the ones that did not believe, and who was the one that would betray him" (6:64). Those who knew the Torah were amazed. "The Jews were astonished at it [Jesus' teaching], saying, "How does this man have such learning, when he has never been taught?" (John 7:15). Even the Jewish police were impressed, despite their leaders. "The police answered, 'Never has anyone spoken like this!'" (7:46).

Many episodes as Jesus entered Jerusalem the final time and after his resurrection are uncanny. Jesus declared, "And I, when I am lifted up from the earth, will draw all peoples to myself" (12:32). This was an astonishing declaration. Who could in good conscience predict that millions in the future would become followers of this uncommon man who was killed in Jerusalem by Roman soldiers as a common criminal? Earlier Jesus had declared, "When you have lifted up the Son of Man, then you will realize that I am he (in the Greek "I am"), and do nothing on my own, but I speak these things as the Father instructed me" (8:28). When Jesus is lifted up those who believe will identify him with the God who appeared to Moses at the burning bush—the great I am

(Exod. 3:14). Peter as the end approached said he would never abandon the Lord and would even lay down his life for him. Jesus responded, "Very truly, I tell you, before the cock crows, you will have denied me three times" (13:38). Peter was so adamant and so sure of himself that his denial of having been with the Lord at once amazes us. But Jesus predicted that Peter would deny the Lord three times and it happened as he declared.

Jesus assured the disciples, "The one who believes in me will do the work that I do and, in fact, will do greater works than these because I am going to the Father" (14:12). Many persons in the future as reported in Acts witnessed such works and came to believe. As Jesus' death approached, his disciples became aware of the growing animosity of the Jewish leaders toward him. They concluded that Jesus was doomed with no recourse. Jesus told them, "So you have pain now; but I will see you again, and your hearts will rejoice, and no one will take that joy from you" (John 16:22). Indeed, the unexpected happened! After expiring on the cross Jesus showed up in a gathering of the disciples. "Then the disciples rejoiced when they saw the Lord" (John 20:20). What greater sign is there that Jesus came from God and is returning to God (John 13:3)? We must also be impressed when Jesus predicted that Peter would die by crucifixion because according to various early Christian writers as Peter faced his death he asked to be placed upside down on the cross for he was not worthy to die in the same manner as his Lord.

Truly all these sayings of and about Jesus are remarkable, unless of course, he has been sent from God and is returning to him. It is to this conclusion that all these signs point.

It wasn't just what Jesus said, but what he did that impressed people. Surely he was not just any roving prophet? As Nicodemus said to Jesus, "Rabbi, we know that you are a teacher who has come from God; for no one can do these signs that you do apart from the presence of God" (John 3:2). In the first specifically described sign, Jesus changed the Jewish water of purification into exceptionally good wine (John 2:10). The sign, however, he offered to the Jewish leaders as the climatic episode that disclosed his origin is his death and resurrection. "The Jews then said to him, 'What sign can you show us for doing this?' Jesus answered them, 'Destroy this temple, and in three days I will raise it up.' The Jews then said, 'This temple has been under construction for forty-six years, and will you raise it up in three days?' But he was speaking of the temple of his body. After he was raised from the dead, his disciples remembered that he had said this; and they believed the scripture and the word that Jesus had spoken" (2:18-22). In another amazing testimony, Jesus said to the royal official whose son was on the point of death "Go; your Son will live" (John 3:50). The official later met his servants on the road and they informed him of the time in which the fever left his son. It was the same moment at which Jesus declared him cured (John 3:53). Not only did the official believe, but also his whole household. "These are written so that you may come to believe that Jesus is the Messiah, the Son of God!"

Jesus followed these early signs with a number of amazing feats. He went to Jerusalem and talked with a man lame and paralyzed who hoped to be healed in the pool of Bethesda. Jesus said to him, "Stand up, take your mat and walk" (John 5:8). And the man infirm for thirty-eight years did so. He took up his mat and began to walk. Because Jesus healed so many, large crowds followed him to an isolated region across the Sea of Galilee. No food was available. The disciples knew of a boy with five barley loaves and two fish. Jesus took the loaves and fish, gave thanks and then started distributing them to more than five thousand people. Everyone ate as much as they wanted and when the remains were taken up they filled twelve baskets (John 6:9-13). That night the disciples got into a boat and rowed across the sea toward Capernaum. In the night a strong wind arose and they were frightened. Then they saw Jesus walking on the water and coming near the boat. They were terrified. When Jesus told them, "Do not be afraid" immediately the boat arrived at the land where they were headed (John 6:16-21).

Later in Jerusalem Jesus saw a blind man as he was walking along. The man was blind from birth. Jesus spate on the ground, made the dust and saliva into a paste, and put it on the blind man's eyes. He then told him to wash in the pool of Siloam. When the blind man returned he could see" (John 9:7). Later the Pharisees tried to get the blind man to denounce Jesus. He assured them, "One thing I do know, that though I was blind, now I see" (John

9:25). In another impressive feat Jesus went to the town of Bethany outside Jerusalem. It was reported to him that Lazarus the brother of Mary and Martha had died. Jesus went toward the village teaching and healing along the way and finally arrived after Lazarus had been dead for four days. After conversing with Mary and Martha, Lazarus's sisters, Jesus walked up to the tomb and cried out to Lazarus in a loud voice, "'Lazarus, come out!' The dead man came out, his hands and feet bound with strips of cloth, and his face wrapped in a cloth. Jesus said to them, 'Unbind him, and let him go'" (John 11:43-44).

The final greatest work of Jesus had to do with his death and resurrection. "I lay down my life in order to take it up again" (John 10:17). After Mary Magdalene, the disciple Jesus loved, and Peter went to the tomb and found it empty, the latter two went away. Mary stayed around and Jesus appeared to her outside the tomb. She didn't know him at first, but he said to her "Mary!" and it dawned on her who it was. Mary was overawed (John 20:16). Jesus later that night appeared to the gathered disciples in a locked room. He entered without disturbing the locks, walls or woodwork (John 20:19). Who then is this who can enter secure rooms? He also appeared to Thomas who was not at the first gathering and the rest of the disciples. He was prepared to let Thomas feel his hands and his side. But Thomas was simply overpowered by his presence and burst out, "My Lord and my God!" (John 20:28). Finally Jesus appeared on the shore of the Sea of Galilee while seven of the disciples were fishing. They had fished through the night and caught nothing. Jesus shouted for them to cast their net on the other side. The outcome was that they caught 153 large fish. The results were so amazing that the disciples knew it could only be Jesus (John 21:1-14). What other conclusion then can one reach but that all the signs point to Jesus as being the Messiah the Son of God?

The Gospel of John provides multiple instances that demonstrate that Jesus is far more than any ordinary man. We need to take up once again the story as John unfolds it. If our faith is commonplace and fragile, the words and works of the Son of God will once again ground our faith in the realities to which the signs in Jesus' words and works point.

My eyes are dry, My faith is old, My heart is hard,
My pray'rs are cold.
And I know how I ought to be, Alive to You and
dead to me.
What can be done to an old heart like mine?
Soften it up with oil and wine.
The oil is You, Your spirit of love. Please wash
me anew in the wine of your blood.

The Gospel disperses the blood from the side of Jesus which poured forth as he hung on the cross into our hearts and quickens and strengthens our faith.

With a newly renewed faith we will go forth to serve, to love, and to feed Christ's sheep. We will be constantly involved in fulfilling the ministry with which Jesus has charged us. We will be led by the *Paraklētos*—the Holy Spirit. We will lift our eyes so as to acknowledge the ministry that is ours. "Those who love their life lose it, and those who hate their life in this world will keep it for eternal life. Whoever serves me must follow me, and where I am, there will my servant be also. Whoever serves me, the Father will honor" (John 12:25-26).

Truly all these sayings of and about
Jesus are remarkable, unless of course,
he has been sent from God
and is returning to him.
It is to this conclusion
that all these signs point.

Bibliography on the Gospel of John

The bibliography on the Gospel of John is enormous. For an up-to-date bibliography of many applicable recent works see the 2003 commentary on John by Keener, pages 1243-1409 of compact, perhaps 11-point type (see the entry below). These may be supplemented with additional specific studies on the Passion narrative in the bibliographies of Brown's *The Death of the Messiah* (see entry below) scattered throughout the two volumes, and a bibliography on the resurrection in Wright's *The Resurrection*, pages 739-779 (see entry below). See also Seán P. Kealy, *John's Gospel and the History of Biblical Interpretation*, 2 vols. Mellen Biblical Press Series 60a, 60b (Lewiston, NY: Mellen, 2002) of almost 1000 pages.

PRIORITIES IN WHAT TO READ

I especially recommend Gail R. O'Day's commentary on the Gospel of John in *The New Interpreter's Bible* (Nashville: Abingdon Press, 1995). This is the best commentary I know for those who preach from the Gospel of John. Her reflection sections are always relevant and suggestive. They may not be the specific applications you need, but they point you in that direction as you rummage through your own resources. It is a bit difficult to imagine a better-rounded commentary. I like it's because O'Day is always sensitive to the special theological developments in the Gospel of John. From reading the commentary you will have good insight into the study of John's Gospel in the last half of the twentieth century. But what is special about this commentary is the manner in which O'Day attempts to look at every detail of the Gospel in the light of the major theological and other trajectories in the Gospel itself. Occasionally her insights as to the special meaning in John are forced and perhaps fanciful. But every observation is worth considering.

I have included here five John commentaries written by

restorationists. Likely the most helpful one is by Frank Pack. I have not examined the recent commentary by Bryant and Krause. These are apparently most of the restorationist commentaries on John. I do not find any produced by major scholars among us though Pack was a scholar of some note. Our scholars have not focused on the Gospels, though probably more on Luke than any of the others. You may be surprised to know the book in the Bible on which the most commentaries have been written by restorationists. I would have guessed Acts. But the answer is Romans. There are some twenty commentaries on Acts and about forty on Romans. Of course, some of these are more study guides than commentaries. I have included the restorationist John commentaries on this list because I think we should give some attention to how these texts have been traditionally treated in our churches. So I encourage you to look at one or more.

ANNOTATED BIBLIOGRAPHY

Barrett, Charles Kingsley. *The Gospel according to St. John: an Introduction with Commentary and Notes on the Greek Text*. 2nd Ed. London: S.P.C.K., 1978. This commentary by a major British commentator, is no doubt the best of the British commentaries. It is often cited by other commentaries for its judicious conclusions and insightful theological suggestions based on the Gospel itself. Barrett was in discussion with C.H. Dodd, the premier British NT scholar of his era who did benchmark studies on John that influenced the international scholarly guild. Unlike more recent scholars, Barrett advocates Johannine dependence on Mark and Luke.

Beasley-Murray, George Raymond. (1916) *John*. 2nd Edition. Nashville: Thomas Nelson Publishers, 1999. Beasley-Murray grew up in England and was trained at Cambridge and the University of London. This commentary is in the Word Commentary series now published by Thomas Nelson. The commentaries in this series, as is this one, are characterized by a critically informed conservatism. The author dialogues with the major commentators on John, in some cases from the patristic period, but he also brings to bear his own considerable scholarship and insight. He teaches at Louisville Baptist Seminary.

Brown, Raymond. *The Death of the Messiah: From Gethsemane to the Grave: A Commentary on the Passion Narratives in the Four Gospels.* 2 Vols. Garden City, NY: Doubleday, 1994. These two lengthy volumes not only discuss the death of Jesus in John, but also in Matthew, Mark and Luke. The volumes are fairly recent. Brown mines most of the major commentaries and studies, but clearly has his own agenda and views. The material from John may be easily located through the index. Brown, an American, was perhaps the major Roman Catholic New Testament scholar in the last half of the twentieth century and his specialty was the Gospel and Epistles of John. His introduction alone is one of the most succinct and sane presentation of scholarly views on the origins of the Gospels and their similarities and differences. His positions are critically informed, but tend to come out in modified traditional positions. His comments tend to be more focused on historicity than theology.

Brown, Raymond. *The Gospel according to John.* 2 Vols. Garden City, NY: Doubleday. 1966. Brown discusses about everything that pertains to and is in the Gospel often in fresh ways. I used to tell students that this is the commentary to read since in it may be found everything you ever wanted to know about the Gospel of John and was afraid to ask.

Bryant, Beauford H., and Mark S. Krause. *John.* College Press NIV Commentary Series. Joplin, MO: College Press, 1998. This is a 400+ commentary. It is worth consulting for standard conventional interpretations. This is the most recent restorationist commentary. The professors have taught in Independent Christian Church Colleges.

Bultmann, Rudolf Karl. *The Gospel of John: a Commentary.* Philadelphia, Westminster Press, 1971. Perhaps Bultmann is the most cited, as often in disagreement as in acquiescence, German New Testament scholar of the last half of the twentieth century. Many interesting and challenging insights are presented in this commentary that continue to be supported especially in regard to theological trajectories. Bultmann set forth views of source documents that may be located in the Gospel. Bultmann taught at the University of Marburg.

Carson, D.A. *The Gospel according to John*. Grand Rapids: W.B. Eerdmans, 1991. This 700+ page work by Carson is cited when conventional more conservative views are sought. Carson is a Professor at Trinity Divinity School, Deerfield, Illinois. In this regard it is now superceded by the more extensive two-volume work by Keener, but it is still worth consulting.

Coffman, James Burton. *Commentary on John*. Austin, TX.: Firm Foundation Publishing House, 1974. Coffman, a Churches of Christ preacher, has published commentaries on all the books of the Bible. The value of this commentary is that Coffman often introduces positions and insights from the old standard quasi-scholarly commentators Matthew Henry, Adam Clark and Albert Barnes.

Culpepper, R. Alan. *The Gospel and Letters of John*. Nashville: Abington Press, 1998. The commentary part of this work is relatively short, but I am impressed with the way in which Culpepper sets out in concrete ways the current thinking on John especially regarding the community implied in the writings, and the literary aspects. The details of the structure and plots may be especially helpful. The tracking of Jesus before Pilate is especially helpful. Culpepper has taught at several Southern Baptist Seminaries and is currently Dean of the McAfee School of Theology, Mercer University. He is middle of the road, and reflects current studies.

Culpepper, R. Alan. *John: The Son of Zebedee: The Life of a Legend*. Minneapolis: Fortress Press, 2000. Culpepper, in this lengthy book (376 pages), starts with the Biblical citations on John, then takes up perspectives on John from the second century to the present. If you are interested in the known and not so well known stories regarding John check them out in this book.

Edwards, Mark J. *John*. Malden, MA: Blackwell Pub., 2004. Edwards, in this most recent short commentary (242 pp.), refers to a rich plethora of remarks on the Gospel with especial attention to the fathers of the church, but all through the centuries to the present. Edwards is a tutor and lecturer in Patristics at Oxford. If you are interested in pithy remarks and sometimes poetry to provide concretion, look for them in this work.

Haenchen, Ernst. *John : a Commentary on the Gospel of John*. Translated by Robert W. Funk. Philadelphia: Fortress Press, 1984. Though in the major Hermeneia commentary series and by a major German scholar, this work is infrequently cited by subsequent scholars. It is especially worth consulting on historical matters.

Johnson, Barton Warren. *John: a Commentary for the People based on both Versions*. St. Louis: Christian Pub. Co., 1886. Johnson was a popular American restorationist commentator of the nineteenth century. He consulted standard works, especially British commentators, and came to his own conclusions. He spent considerable time harmonizing the passion narratives in John with those in the Synoptics. He is normally a quick read, and these 326 pages are worth perusing.

Keener, Craig S. *The Gospel of John: A Commentary*. 2 Vols. Peabody: Hendrickson Publishers, 2003. Keener is Professor of New Testament at Eastern Theological seminary. His two-volume work of 1635 pages has raised the bar for basically conservative scholarship on John. He has looked at everyone regardless where they are located on the theological spectrum. He has also brought considerable new material to bear on the gospel from ancient extra-Biblical references, the blurb on the back claiming more than 20,000. It is not difficult to generate such references these days with the digitization of ancient texts and efficient search engines. One wonders if Keener checked all of these out himself. But on occasion he evaluates the references as to the insights they may bring to bear on John. I am impressed with the way the commentary is laid out. It is easy to find desired sections. Keener discusses the standard and appropriate questions. He does not get the creative juices going in the manner of O'Day. But this commentary is well worth the read. Keener apprenticed on John under the American doyen of Johannine studies, D. Moody Smith (see below).

Kysar, Robert. *John*. Minneapolis, MN: Augsburg Pub. House, 1986. Kysar, an American Lutheran has written several insightful pieces on the Gospel of John. This relatively short commentary is useful, but not detailed.

Kysar, Robert. *The Maverick Gospel*. Atlanta: John Knox, 1976. In my early days of teaching the theology of John, I was impressed with the manner in which Kysar set forth the distinctives of John in this volume as is noted by the title. I was also impressed by his views regarding the way in which signs lead persons to faith. He has an excellent perspective on signs as to whether they lead to faith or detract from it. Later commentaries have not followed his insights as much as they might have.

Lindars, Barnabas. *The Gospel of John*. London: Oliphants, 1972. Lindars, a noted British scholar in his time, has written a solid, conventional commentary on the Gospel.

Lipscomb, David. (1831-1917) *A Commentary on the Gospel by John*. Nashville: Gospel Advocate Co., 1939. This is a commentary put together from David Lipscomb's writings on John and edited by J.W. Shepherd and C.E.W. Dorris. Some of the comments in this 339-page commentary are interesting.

MacRae, George W. *Invitation to John: a commentary on the Gospel of John with complete text from the Jerusalem Bible*. Garden City, NJ: Image Books, 1978. George MacRae was a major Roman Catholic New Testament scholar who taught at Harvard. This is a short commentary, but has interesting reflections on the structure of John and the relationships of John to Gnosticism.

Malina, Bruce J., and Richard L. Rohrbaugh. *Social-science Commentary on the Gospel of John*. Minneapolis: Fortress Press, 1998. These American New Testament scholars are noted for applying the insights of sociological models to NT documents. They have a special interest in crowds and locations. The comments in this volume are rather short, but a few worthwhile insights may be obtained for those interested in these matters. They bring to bear certain ancient details of locations that may not be found elsewhere.

Morris, Leon. (1914) *The Gospel according to John*. Rev. Ed. Grand Rapids: W.B. Eerdmans Pub. Co., 1995. Morris is a conservative British scholar of some note. His reflections are rather standard, but of considerable length (900+ pages). He discusses the views of current scholars and has some helpful insights of his own.

Pack, Frank. *The Gospel according to John*. 2 Vols. Abilene, TX: Abilene Christian University, A.C.U. Press, 1984. Pack was the most noted Johannine scholar in Churches of Christ having taught in graduate programs at Abilene Christian and Pepperdine. These commentaries are in the Living Word Series. These may be especially helpful for preaching on these texts.

Ridderbos, Herman N. *The Gospel according to John: a Theological Commentary*. Translated by John Vriend. Grand Rapids: W.B. Eerdmans Pub., 1997. Ridderbos is a recognized Dutch scholar. This commentary is good on theology and historical backgrounds.

Schnackenburg, Rudolf. *The Gospel according to St. John*. 3 Vols. Translated by Cecily Hastings, Francis McDonagh, David Smith, and Richard Foley. New York: Crossroads, 1990. Schnackenburg is a major German Roman Catholic New Testament Scholar. This three-volume commentary is well written and balanced. He examines many works available up to the time the commentaries were published. Schnackenburg should be consulted on any text under consideration.

Smith, D. Moody. *John*. Nashville: Abingdon Press, 1999. Moody Professor of New Testament at Duke, has been in the forefront of the history of Johannine studies for thirty-five years. He trained many of the publishing scholars on Johannine documents. This is a rather short commentary, but Smith has packed in much pointed, succinct information. His comments in this commentary will be helpful for a quick review of John 18–21.

Smith, D. Moody. *The Theology of the Gospel of John*. Cambridge: Cambridge University Press, 1995. This work is an excellent introduction to the theology of the Gospel. Moody uses as his categories those that come from the Gospel itself.

Talbert, Charles H. *Reading John: a Literary and Theological Commentary on the Fourth Gospel and the Johannine Epistles*. New York: Crossroads, 1992. Talbert, an American Southern Baptist, is an expert on the Gospels, especially Luke. He is good at setting forth major structures and how they reflect the major theological themes. This is a short commentary of 284 pages, which includes comments on the Johannine epistles. Talbert teaches at Baylor University.

Witherington, Ben. *John's Wisdom: a Commentary on the Fourth Gospel*. 1st Ed. Louisville, KY: Westminster John Knox Press, 1995. Witherington is a basically conservative commentator who has now published major commentaries on several New Testament books. Witherington is good on backgrounds and structures. This is a 400+ page commentary.

Woods, Guy N. *A Commentary on the Gospel according to John*. Nashville, TN: Gospel Advocate Co., 1981. Guy Woods was a popular Churches of Christ debater and preacher. He was good at certain practical observations and noticing structures useful for preaching.

Wright, N.T. *The Resurrection of the Son of God*. Minneapolis: Fortress Press, 2003. The work of Raymond Brown on the death of the Messiah did not continue into John 20 on the resurrection. This work will be of help on chapter 20. The index will indicate appropriate sections of the book to examine. This is a major and significant work by an important British scholar.

About the Author

Thomas H. Olbricht grew up in Thayer, Missouri. He attended Harding University, Northern Illinois University, The University of Iowa and Harvard Divinity School. He studied Scripture, communication, and church history. He has taught at Harding University, The University of Dubuque and its Theological Seminary, The Pennsylvania State University, Abilene Christian University, and is Distinguished Professor Emeritus of Religion at Pepperdine University.

He has authored or edited sixteen books along with numerous essays in books and in periodicals. Along the way he has served as minister in several Churches of Christ, and has preached or lectured on every continent except for Antarctica.

He lives in retirement in South Berwick, Maine, along with his wife Dorothy. They have been married for fifty-four years and have five children and twelve grandchildren.